OUR FATHERS AND US
The Heritage of the Methodists

By Umphrey Lee

JESUS THE PIONEER

A SHORT SKETCH OF THE LIFE OF CHRIST

THE LORD'S HORSEMAN: JOHN WESLEY THE MAN

THE BIBLE AND BUSINESS

HISTORICAL BACKGROUNDS OF EARLY METHODIST
ENTHUSIASM

JOHN WESLEY AND MODERN RELIGION

THE HISTORIC CHURCH AND MODERN PACIFISM

RENDER UNTO THE PEOPLE

A SHORT HISTORY OF METHODISM
with William Warren Sweet

OUR FATHERS
AND US

THE HERITAGE OF THE METHODISTS

Umphrey Lee

With a Memorial Preface by
Herbert Gambrell

SOUTHERN METHODIST UNIVERSITY PRESS, DALLAS

1958

*The material in this book, with the exception
of Chapter Five, originated in somewhat
different form as the 1957 Fondren Lectures
at Southern Methodist University.*

The Library of Congress has catalogued this book as
follows:

LEE, UMPHREY, 1893-1958.
   Our fathers and us; the heritage of the Methodists.
Dallas, Southern Methodist University Press, 1958.

   123 p.   23 cm.

   Includes bibliography.

   1. Methodism.   I. Title.

BX8331.L43   287   58–14109 ‡

Library of Congress

UMPHREY LEE, 1893-1958

A Memorial Preface

THE MAN who for nearly half a century was the living symbol of Southern Methodist University died in his office on the campus on June 23, 1958. His career was marvelously interwoven with that of the institution which knew him successively as student, teacher, president, and chancellor. He came to Texas when the creation of the university was still in the discussion stage. Before it opened its doors, he had his undergraduate education at two Presbyterian colleges — one southern, Daniel Baker; the other northern, Trinity — where the curriculum was old-fashioned, classical, and solid.

He entered the new School of Theology September 22, 1915, as a graduate student, candidate for the master's degree; but he studied the humanities more than formal theology. With prophetic wisdom the student body elected him its first president. He helped create college traditions.

Briefly he was a youthful pastor at Cisco and Ennis, but the campus, not First Church, was where he belonged. In 1919 he was in Austin establishing the Wesley Bible Chair at the University of Texas. His courses were credited in the Department of English.

In 1923 he was back on the Southern Methodist University campus as pastor of the college-community church that was worshiping in a little brown frame building overshadowed by the imposing new stadium. Here he disproved the theory that a minister can appeal to businessmen and professional men, or he can attract students and intellectuals, but he cannot do both simultaneously. For thirteen years he preached to ever increasing congregations. He designed the Gothic sanctuary of Highland Park Methodist Church and got it built; he served the university as professor of homiletics and the community in many capacities; but he also found time to complete his doctorate in history at Columbia, and to travel abroad.

Next he spent three years rebuilding Vanderbilt University's School of Religion, serving as Dean and Drucilla Moore Buffington Professor of Church History. From this fruitful and relatively secluded employment he was plunged into the presidency of his alma mater. The institution was in its twenty-fifth year and he entered on his duties, like Woodrow Wilson at Washington in 1913, with some definite notions of what he should do; but his term of office, like that of this great President of the United States, was beset with problems other than those he had prepared himself to cope with. But like Wilson, he demonstrated capacities that his friends had not suspected. He was no money-raiser, he said, and they believed him; but at the end of fifteen years $20,500,000 had been added to the university's resources and eighteen new buildings were on the campus. Modestly and with a degree of truth he asserted that others, not he, induced the gifts; but the fact remains that most of these benefactions came to the university because he was there.

He planned educational reforms that were only partially effected because of the world crises that brought first scant, then swollen, enrolments and a multitude of vexatious problems. But continually he held before himself and his faculties the goal of an institution of higher learning that commanded the respect of its sisters and occasionally blazed a new trail.

A man of rare and contradictory qualities, Umphrey Lee approximated the Pauline ideal of being all things to all men. His tastes were catholic — in people as well as in literature and aesthetics. An amazing cross-section of humanity counted him friend and leaned on him for counsel on every conceivable subject. He loved humanity in the aggregate and in the individual specimen. He had an uncanny, intuitive understanding of the other fellow's point of view and sometimes a baffling appreciation of his crotchets. Any situation in which he found himself evoked from him the unstudied response of a mind stored with wisdom as well as learning, controlled by a heart that evaluated sympathetically the human factors involved, conveyed by a tongue that used language to express, not to obscure, thought. No man of his generation was more eagerly sought as speaker, dinner guest, or companion.

He was a man of principle, but his principles never drove him to monomania. He was a professor of history and a historian of distinction, and history taught him that time is on the side of Truth and that patience, even with wrong-headedness, is a virtue. He was fortunate to have had a father of pioneer mold, an uncompromising fighter against every error, eager to "take a stand" on every current question in religion, economics, or politics. He admired his father's spirit and his integrity but he did not emulate his technique. The son never fought if the desired end could be attained otherwise. If a fight was inevitable, he could hit hard; but fighting never exhilarated him.

He had a contagious sense of humor and—what is rarer—a Shavian wit, which enabled him to see all things (including himself) in just proportion. He had little of what we call personal vanity, but he evaluated himself with an accurate sense of his own capacities.

Maybe the circumstances of his life account for many of the facets of his complex personality. Brought up in the parsonage of an intense preacher-father who did not join the Methodists until he was near sixty, trained in rigidly Calvinistic colleges, he became one of the great interpreters of Arminian tradition and of the Wesleyan movement. His works are as well known in England as in this country. Never a student of formal theology, he became successively a distinguished professor, dean, and president of theological seminaries. A "small-town preacher" of only local reputation, he became the most evocative sermonizer of an urban metropolis. A man inexperienced in large-scale finance and administration, he quickly became an educational statesman whose advice was followed by men of longer and more varied experience.

In every relationship of life, in every task to which he set his hand, Umphrey Lee was an extraordinary man. He was an integral and vital part of Southern Methodist University from its opening day until his death forty-three years later; and more than any other person he molded it into its present form and brought it to its present stature. It is literally his monument set upon a hill.

Such a man is History; his work is Heritage.

HERBERT GAMBRELL

Southern Methodist University
September 15, 1958

CONTENTS

OUR FATHERS AND US
The Heritage of the Methodists

CHAPTER ONE

WHY WE ARE AS WE ARE

AMONG the missionary enterprises of modern times, the Methodist movement has been unquestionably the greatest in number of people affected and territory covered. At the beginning of the last century so fixed was the notion that Methodism was a missionary movement that the proposal to organize a missionary society in the Methodist church in the United States was opposed by many on the ground that the church itself was a missionary movement. Today Methodist churches cannot be distinguished in many essentials from churches of other Protestant denominations. They undertake the "cure of souls"; they are concerned with the public worship of God; they administer the recognized sacraments: in short, they are not only preaching places, but churches. Yet there are certain peculiarities of organization and of worship which can be understood only when considered in the light of the history of the Methodist movement.

The primary fact in the history of this movement that we now call the Methodist church is that, alone among the larger Protestant denominations, Methodism did not begin as a protest against the church to which its founders belonged. It began as a definite effort to bring people into communion with the church from which it later separated. Methodism grew up criticizing its mother church and desiring to show it the way more truly; and all the time the Methodist leaders insisted that they were simply teaching what they called "the good old Church of England doctrine."

In recent years Dr. Leslie F. Church has maintained that the people of the Methodist church really determined its course. This is true, particularly after the death of John and Charles Wesley. But so long as the Wesleys lived, John in particular kept a directing hand on the movement; and, while he may have realized that the people who had come into the Methodist Societies were not going to remain in the Church of England, this seems to have made little difference to him in his attempts to chart his course. The Wesleys attempted to deepen and to correct the religious life of the church which they loved, but they never wavered in their loyalty to it. It is true that there are times when one wonders if John Wesley realized the consequences of some of the things he did; but there is no question about what he himself thought he was doing.

The doctrines which Wesley preached he sincerely believed to be the genuine doctrines of the Church of England. It is true that loyal members of the Church of England did not believe this to be correct, but apparently Wesley did. When he was seventy-four years old he laid the cornerstone of City Road Chapel in London. This was a solemn occasion, as the Chapel and the buildings around it were the headquarters of Methodism in the three kingdoms. On that occasion Wesley took the opportunity to say some things about the doctrine of Methodism which are worth remembering:

And this is the religion of the Church of England; as appears from all her authentic records, from the uniform tenor of her Liturgy, and from numberless passages in her Homilies. The scriptural, primitive religion of love, which is now reviving throughout the three kingdoms, is to be found in our a.m. and e.s., and in their daily, as well as occasional, Prayers; and the whole of it is beautifully summed up in that comprehensive petition, "cleanse the thoughts of our hearts by the inspiration of the Holy Spirit, that we may perfectly love thee, and worthily magnify thy holy name."[1]

What did Wesley intend? In the address which contains the passage quoted above, Wesley stated what he considered to be the beginning of the Methodist Society in England. He recalls that when he returned to England at the beginning of February, 1738, he was in haste to retire to Oxford to bury himself "in my beloved obscurity." He was, however, detained in London week after week by the trustees for the colony of Georgia.

In the meantime, I was continually importuned to preach in one and another church; and that not only morning, afternoon, and night, on Sunday, but on week days also. As I was lately come from a far country, vast multitudes flocked together; but in a short time, partly because of those unwieldy crowds, partly because of my unfashionable doctrine, I was excluded from one and another church, and, at length, shut out of all! Not daring to be silent after a short struggle between honor and conscience, I made a virtue of necessity, and preached in the middle of Moorfields. Here were thousands upon thousands, abundantly more than any church could contain; and numbers among them, who never went to any church or place of public worship at all. More and more of them were cut to the heart, and came to me all in tears inquiring, with the utmost eagerness, what they must do to be saved. . . . Thus, without a previous plan or design, began the Methodist Society in England—a company of people associating together, to help each other to work out their own salvation.[2]

To carry on his missionary work, John Wesley organized societies. These societies made possible in a very real sense a cure of souls, a preservation of the results of missionary preaching. But the creation of societies which were not churches, but were considered as complementary to the church, has left an indelible mark upon Methodism wherever it has been continued. Many of the differences which mark off Methodism from other Christian churches are derived from its origin as a society supplementary and complementary to a church, rather than as a church that is founded in opposition to the existing body.

There are certain inheritances of Methodists which come to them because Methodism began as a society which, by the Wesleys at least, was intended to remain within the Church of England. One of these results is that the Methodist church to which we belong has no creedal requirement for its members. The Rules of the United Societies, which remained in force when the Methodist church was organized, state definitely: "There is one only condition previously required in those who desire admission into these Societies, a desire to flee from the wrath to come, to be saved from their sins." It is probable, as John S. Simon believes, and as the Rules now read, that Wesley intended this condition to be read as: "A desire to flee from the wrath to come and to be saved from their sins."[3]

It would be foolish to suppose that John Wesley, a clergyman of the Church of England, meant by this rule that those who came into the Methodist Societies should have no conditions so far as their beliefs were concerned. What he actually meant can be seen from his words in *The Character of a Methodist:*

The distinguishing marks of a Methodist are not, his opinions of any sort. His assenting to this or that scheme of religion, his embracing any particular set of notions, his espousing the judgment of one man or of another, are all quite wide of the point. Whosoever therefore imagines, that a Methodist is, a man of such and such an opinion, is grossly ignorant of the whole affair; he mistakes the truth totally.

If one were to take this as it stands it would be difficult to imagine a more open door to all sorts and conditions of men. But Wesley had a definite idea as to what "opinions" were. He continues in his description of the character of a Methodist:

We believe indeed, that all scripture is given by the inspiration of God, and herein we are distinguished from Jews, Turks, and Infidels. We believe the written word of God to be the only and sufficient rule, both of Christian faith and practice; and herein we are fundamentally distinguished from those of the Romish church. We believe Christ to be the eternal supreme God; and herein we are distinguished from the Socinians and Arians. But as to all opinions which do not strike at the root of Christianity, we think and let think so that whatsoever they are, whether right or wrong, they are no distinguishing marks of a Methodist.

It is obvious that there were certain beliefs which Wesley expected of his people. They were assumptions which he did not question and did not expect his people to question. He was not himself a speculative theologian, and he usually reacted to theological controversies in a "common-sense" way.

He believed most heartily in the Trinity, but he would not contend for the term. He thought that Servetus (who was burned in Geneva) was not really anti-Trinitarian, although he dared not use the words "Trinity" or "Person." "I dare," commented Wesley, "and I think them very good words. But I should think it very hard to be burned alive for not using them; especially with a slow fire, made of moist, green wood."[4]

Wesley is still more specific in discussing the doctrine of Justification by Faith. He put it in a fashion which makes the question a living one. "If a doctrine like Justification by Faith must be believed in order for one to have salvation, what becomes of the good man, the obviously Christian man, who doesn't believe in it, e.g. William Law?" Now there was a quality of concreteness in Wesley's thinking, which is the characteristic of a manager, the man who arranges things and people; and while this is not the quality which makes philosophers and theologians, it is that which keeps them from drifting off into the clouds. When you state the problem of the essentialness of an article of a creed in this fashion, your answer must be that such and such a man is or is not destined for hell as an unbeliever. Wesley answered his question in his *Journal* on December 1, 1767:

It appeared "clear as day" that "a mystic, who denies Justification by Faith (Mr. Law for instance) may be saved." But from the specific one must go on to the general. If William Law can be saved, "What becomes of *articulus stantis vel cadentis ecclesiae?*" If Law can be saved, "is it not high time for us to 'reject bombast and words half a yard long,' and to return to the plain word, 'he that feareth God and worketh righteousness, is accepted of Him'?"[5]

While Wesley did have assumptions concerning Christian doctrine, and it would have been impossible for anyone to belong to his Societies and accept the Rules without assenting to basic Christian doctrines, it remains true that Wesley's "one only" rule for admission to the Societies was startling in its day and has been startling since that time. But he did not allow his preachers the liberty that he allowed members in the Society. The Rules of the Societies and the provisions in the deeds for his chapels made it very evident that preachers were supposed to subscribe to the doctrines that were taken to be Methodistic and to the interpretations of Wesley as set down in his *Standard Sermons* and in his *Notes on the New Testament.*

One of the practical results of this admission without subscription to creeds was that dissenters gradually became members of the Societies. A further result of this was that the Methodist Societies themselves no longer were primarily interested in remaining in the Church of England. Thus, Wesley's own provision made for the final abrogation of the rule to which he clung during his lifetime: that the Societies should remain within the Church of England.

Nevertheless, he boasted to the end that his Societies did not require subscription to those theological doctrines which Wesley believed to be "opinions." In Glasgow in the last years of his life he declared to a congregation:

There is no other religious society under Heaven which requires nothing of men in order to their admission into it but a desire to save souls. Look all around you; you cannot be admitted into the Church, or society of the Presbyterians, Anabaptists, Quakers, or any other unless you hold the same opinion with them, and adhere to the same mode of worship. The Methodists alone do not insist on your holding this or that opinion; but they think and let think. Neither do they impose any particular mode of worship, be it what it may. Now, I do not know any other religious society, either ancient or modern, wherein such liberty of conscience is now allowed or has been allowed since the age of the Apostles. Here is our glorying; and a glorying peculiar to us. What Society shares it with us?

Another inheritance from the Societies is in the General Rules and the conception of the religious life as one

that must be governed by rules. The so-called General
Rules which were formerly required to be read at stated
times to every congregation are of course the rules of
the "United Societies" which were taken over by the
Methodist church.

In order to refresh our memories it may be well to
recall that section of the General Rules which specifies
certain things that Methodists are not to do. After setting forth the "one only" condition previously required
of those who desire admission to the Societies, the General Rules set forth some of the things that must be done
in order to show that the members desire salvation:

First, by doing no harm; by avoiding evil in every kind;
especially that which is most generally practiced. Such is:
    The taking the name of God in vain;
    The profaning the Day of the Lord, either by doing ordi-
nary work thereon, or by buying or selling;
    Drunkenness, buying or selling spirituous liquors; or
drinking them (unless in cases of extreme necessity);
    Fighting, quarreling, brawling; going to law; returning
evil for evil or railing for railing; the using many words in
buying or selling;
    The buying or selling uncustomed goods;
    The giving or taking things on usury;
    Uncharitable or unprofitable conversation;
    Doing to others as we would not they should do unto us;
    Doing what we know is not for the glory of God: as the
putting on of gold, or costly apparel; the taking such diversions as cannot be used in the name of the Lord Jesus;
    The singing those songs, or the reading those books, which
do not tend to the knowledge or love of God;
    Softness, and needless self-indulgence;
    Laying up treasures upon earth.

It might be well at the beginning to make it clear that
these rules are not simply an inheritance from the Puritanism of the seventeenth century. For some strange

reason it is assumed by many that wherever there are rules for the religious life, particularly wherever there are rules that forbid worldly amusements or worldly indulgence, these are necessarily inheritances from what we have come to call Puritanism.

The late Professor G. C. Coulton of Cambridge insisted upon the "Puritanism" of the Middle Ages. In answering those critics of Protestantism who insisted that the joy of life which had been affirmed by the Catholic faith had been blotted out by the Protestant teaching, Coulton brought forward evidence of the attitude of medieval moralists toward amusements, dress, and the lighter side of life. Indeed, Coulton quotes the great seventeenth-century French Catholic preacher, Massillon, in a statement that almost parallels that of the General Rules: "Everything we do, everything we rejoice or weep at, ought to be of such a nature as to have a connexion with Jesus Christ, and to be done to His glory."[6] This statement appears in a paragraph in which Massillon is attacking the theater.

This is indeed the statement that almost all writers, whether mystics or of a monastic turn, or simply devotional writers, make when they are trying to define the attitude of the truly religious person. We should remember that John Wesley attributed his awakening in 1725 largely to the reading of Thomas à Kempis' *The Imitation of Christ*, Bishop Jeremy Taylor's *Holy Living and Holy Dying*, and William Law's *Christian Perfection*. It should be pointed out that Thomas à Kempis was a medieval Catholic; that Bishop Jeremy Taylor was a High-Church bishop of the seventeenth-century Church of England; that William Law was a High-Churchman whose conscience was so tender that he was not willing to take the oath of allegiance after the Revolution of 1688. *Christian Perfection*, the book which Wesley

cherished all his life, although he later had disputes with
its author, makes it very clear that "not only the vices,
the wickedness and vanity of this world, but even its
most lawful and allowed concerns, render men unable
to enter, and unworthy to be received into the true
state of Christianity."[7] He makes it clear also that Christians must be indifferent about raiment and about food.
One of the better known of his works, written at about
the same time as *Christian Perfection,* was *The Absolute Unlawfulness of the Stage-Entertainment Fully
Demonstrated.*

The point of view which William Law held, and
which has been held by generations of Christians
whether Puritan or Catholic, was stated by Law in his
famous book, *A Serious Call to a Devout and Holy Life:*

The short of the matter is this, either reason and religion pre-
scribe rules and ends to all the ordinary actions of our life,
or they do not: if they do, then it is as necessary to govern
all our actions by those rules as it is necessary to worship
God. For if religion teaches us anything concerning eating
and drinking, or spending our time and money, if it teaches
us how we are to use and contemn the world, if it tells us
what tempers we are to have in common life, how we are to
be disposed towards all people, how we are to behave
toward the sick, the poor, the old and destitute; if it tells us
who we are to treat with a particular love . . . he must be
very weak, that can think these parts of religion are not to
be observed with as much exactness, as any doctrines that
relate to prayers.

Circumstances under which Methodism progressed
in the New World aided this emphasis on rules and
regulations. There is no question that in the frontier
society in which Methodism found itself more and more
in the New World, the regulations which had been
inherited from the religious society called Methodist

were of great help. A backwoods Irish schoolmaster said
in Eggleston's *The Circuit Rider:*

Now, the Mithodists air a narry sort of a payple. But if you
want to make a strame strong you hav to make it narry.
I've read a good dale of history, and in me own estimation
the ould Anglish Puritans and the Mithodists air both tor-
rents, because they're both shet up by narry banks. The
Mithodists is ferninst the wearin' of jewelry and dancin' and
singin' songs which is all vairy foolish in me own estimation.
But it's kind o' nat'ral for the millrace that turns the whale
that fades the worruld to git mad at the babblin', oidle brook
that wastes its toime among the mossy shtones and grinds
nobody's grist.[8]

The rules by which the Methodists were supposed to
live were Society Rules. They were not derived merely
from the Puritans, although in the public mind the
Puritans are identified today with opposition to amuse-
ment and with the forbidding of many presumed
pleasures. But John Wesley had lived by rules in his
mother's house. High-Churchwoman as she was, she
was a person of method. Wesley had imbibed from the
High-Church and Catholic sources which he had read
in his early days as a student the belief in living by
rule. John Wesley's father had approved of the Religious Societies of his day, and had taken part in the
Society for the Reformation of Manners, which, among
other things, set itself to have enforced statutes against
public swearing and Sabbath-breaking. All this was
translated into the rules of the Societies.

An examination of the General Rules might astonish
some people today: not only do they embody provisions
which are not known now, but other provisions which
everyone seems to have taken for granted from the
beginning as being a part of the Methodist Discipline
are conspicuous by their absence. It is to be noted

that Wesley speaks of avoiding evil, especially that
which is most generally practiced. Under this he
puts things like Sabbath-breaking and swearing, fighting and going to law. But he also includes the buying and selling of goods that have not paid the duty.
He includes giving or taking things on usury (probably in his definition of "usury" following the medieval notion that *all* interest is usurious). He includes
among practices forbidden the putting on of gold
or costly apparel, which in the eighteenth century
would have affected men as much as women.

The prohibitions in the General Rules are really not
as biting as Law's statement:

A lady abominates a sot as a creature that has only the
shape of a man; but then she does not consider that drunken
as he is, perhaps he can be more content with the want
[lack] of liquor than she can be with the want [lack] of
fine clothes.[9]

The Methodist attitude toward novels, dances, card-
playing, and attendance at the theater are covered in
the General Rules only by the provision that one should
not take such diversions as cannot be used in the name
of the Lord Jesus, nor read such books nor sing such
songs as do not tend to the knowledge or love of God.

Actually Wesley had stricter rules for some of his
people. But in dealing with the majority he would not
let his preachers say more about some of these things
than that "some may do these things but I can not."
Wesley said that to say more would condemn his own
father and mother. They, for example, had brought a
dancing teacher into their home to instruct the children.
Wesley himself said that he wished he could have one
for his preachers long enough to teach them to get in
and out of a room. As to novels, Wesley could not fol-

low his own rules. He abridged and published one famous novel of his day; he probably mangled it.

The rules against softness and needless self-indulgence and against laying up treasures upon earth are simply Wesley's protest against what Law called "full, fat and stately Christians."[10] This must be read in the light of Wesley's own principle: "Make all you can; save all you can; give all you can."

It was admissible in the Methodists to make money if they gave it away: but as they followed the doctrine of work and thrift, their increasing prosperity became more and more a problem that plagued Wesley. The Quakers had the same experience earlier. As the Methodists became more truly Methodists in their economic life, they made money. As they made money, they tended to lay up treasures. As they laid up treasures, they became less and less interested in their souls. It is a development that has repeated itself more than once in Christian history.

Methodism was from first to last governed by the Wesleys' doctrine of Christian Perfection. This was their goal in Oxford; this was their goal when the shadows closed over them in the latter part of the century. The Rules by which they would guide those who sought to work out their salvation were not simply rules to prevent them from going to hell, but rules to help them come closer to the ideal of inward and outward holiness. As such they are similar to the rules by which the saints have guided themselves in all ages. We have quoted only from the Rules about what *not* to do. The other positive Rules, about what to do, including the using of the Means of Grace, make this clearer. But there is a danger when the Rules are given as a way of life.

For one thing, time goes on and some of the Rules become outmoded. Wesley was concerned with an

issue burning in some parts of England and dangerous
to deal with: smuggling. Today it is unlikely many
Methodists live in areas where this is a problem. His
rules on strong drink are a little out of date. A promi-
nent American Methodist bishop told me once that,
when he was connected with the Board of Temperance
of the Methodist Church, he never allowed John Wesley or his mother to be quoted. Their problems were
different. Though gin and liquors formed one of the
great evils of the day, the habits of centuries (combined
with the lack of pure water supplies) allowed the use
of other types of alcoholic beverages.

If the prohibitions against gold and costly apparel
and against the singing of songs or the reading of books
which Wesley would have thought not conducive to
strengthening one's love of God were strictly enforced,
there would be few Methodist preachers and fewer
Methodist laymen left. What happens when rules are
outgrown or become impossible to keep, either because
they go too far or because they do not go far enough,
is too often that some small rule is exalted out of proportion, or a new rule is invented. As these become the
measure of spirituality, the entire intent of the original
rules is lost.

Another result of the fact that Methodism began as
Societies supplementary to a church is the use of what
were first called lay-assistants or lay-helpers. These were
the lay preachers who were employed to help the
Wesleys as the work became too much for them to carry
on alone. Wesley took the step of employing these lay
helpers with a great deal of hesitation, and is reported
to have authorized his first lay preacher at the urging
of his mother. This was not to be construed as the
ordaining of a minister but as the employing of a person who was to do a certain limited amount of work.

In recent years a great deal of attention has been paid by historians to the early Methodist preachers. They were not a set of ignorant men, as is too frequently supposed. A number of them qualified for admission into the priesthood of the established church. Many of them were men of considerable education. The provisions that Wesley himself made for the training of his preachers were themselves of no little importance. But it is to be understood that Wesley definitely limited them as to the work they were to do. In John Bennett's copy of the Minutes of the early conferences, the rules of an Assistant shed a good deal of light upon the restrictions that Wesley put upon the preachers. In addition to those which are embodied in our own charges to young ministers, there are some phrases that have been changed. For example: "Be serious. Let your motto be, Holiness unto the Lord. Avoid all lightness as you would avoid hell-fire, and laughing as you would cursing and swearing."

This latter phrase perhaps explains the assumption so frequently made that the Methodists were a sour people. On the other hand, one of Wesley's preachers complained that Wesley himself moved his companions to levity. The point is, of course, that Wesley gave strict instructions for his preachers in order that they might do their work and avoid the buffoonery that was so frequently thought of by ignorant enemies when they spoke of Methodist preachers. A further rule for an Assistant was: "Take no money of anyone. If they give you food when you are hungry, or clothes when you need them, it is good, but not silver or gold. Let there be no pretense to say, we grow rich by the Gospel."

At the very time when Wesley was making these provisions—no one doubts that he was the one who did it

—he was receiving his stipend as a Fellow of Lincoln College. While he felt that there was extravagance and ostentation in the church to which he belonged, nevertheless he did not at all raise his voice against the fact that the clergy of the Church of England received their living from the church. His only provision was that Methodist preachers who were called out to do an extraordinary work should not be salaried men. They were not ministers, they were lay preachers.

From this, however, came a tradition in Methodism, particularly in American Methodism, that was many years in passing. Methodism's record in education has been good; but there were many years when the Methodist church distrusted preachers who were college graduates.

At the time there was good reason for this, since it was feared that a man who had an education unusual for those days would not be willing to undergo the hardships necessary for a Methodist preacher on the frontier. And this fear was probably justified. In any case, our inheritance from the Societies persisted for many years. It is only within the memory of many of us that educational requirements have been raised to anything like the present level.

To a certain extent also the Methodist church has inherited from the Societies a form of government. I refer here to the method by which appointments are made, and by which power in the Methodist church is centered either in one man or in a group of men. Dr. Leslie F. Church, in his excellent books on the Methodist people, has made the point well that the form Methodism took in England and elsewhere has been to a large extent due to the Methodist people themselves. There is no question of this, nor is there any question that in the Methodist church certain powers have been reserved either to the bishops or to the preachers, and that the reservation of these powers is the result of the way in which the Methodist church originated.

As the Societies were formed under the direction of the Wesleys, so the work progressed under their direction. It is very doubtful whether the work could have gone on either in England or in America unless there had been strong hands to take care of it. It is very true that Wesley had the ability to govern, and his handling of the Methodist Societies is also a tribute to his power of management. Left rudderless they would have been absorbed as so many other religious groups were absorbed, either by the Church of England or by dissenting bodies. Wesley himself was well aware of the power that he exercised. He knew very well that the lay preachers whom he admitted to be his helpers were men who could not work without direction; and he realized, too, that if he once admitted others of the clergy of the Church of England to take charge of his work it would assume forms different at least from those which he himself intended.

A reading of the Minutes which set forth Wesley's reasons and his understanding of his power is illuminating. In the Large Minutes Wesley explains that the first men who came to him desiring to help him in the Gospel, Thomas Maxfield and Thomas West Richards and Thomas Westell, desired to serve him as sons and "to labor when and where I should direct." Here, he said, commenced his power to determine when and where and how these assistants should labor. In 1744, continued Wesley, he wrote to several clergymen and asked them if they would serve as sons in the Gospel. Some of them agreed so to do, but Wesley pointed out that they came of their own free choice. He sent for them to advise, not to govern him.

When he comes to define his power, Wesley is very explicit:

What is that power? It is a power of admitting into, and excluding from, the Societies under my care; of choosing and removing stewards; of receiving or not receiving helpers; of appointing them when, where, and how to help me, and of desiring any of them to confer with me when I see good. And as it was merely in obedience to the providence of God, and for the good of the people, that I at first accepted this power, which I never sought; so it is on the same consideration, not for profit, honour, or pleasure, that I use it at this day. . . .

But some of our helpers say "This is shackling free-born Englishmen;" and demand a free Conference, that is, a meeting of all the preachers, wherein all things shall be determined by most votes. I answer it is possible, after my death, something of this kind may take place; but not while I live. . . .

It is nonsense, then, to call my using this power "shackling free-born Englishmen." None needs to submit to it unless he wills; so that there is no shackling in the case. Every preacher and every member may leave me when he pleases. But while he chooses to stay, it is on the same terms that he joined me at first.[11]

In another connection I have pointed out, as have Methodist historians elsewhere, that the Methodist organization was peculiarly fitted for the American continent. It made it possible for Methodists to be sent to every corner of this country. And it was this constant supervision that caused Methodists to appear in every part of what is now called the United States.

If the Methodist church had begun as a church, it would have contained many features which the Wesleys themselves would not have approved. Methodism might well have begun without the Wesleys, but it would not have been the Methodism that we know.

It is perhaps well for the history of religion that Methodism did begin under the supervision of two clergymen of the Church of England, and that it was necessary to employ lay preachers and to carry on the work as it was carried on. It was certainly inevitable that Methodism so begun and so carried on could not remain as an auxiliary to eighteenth-century Anglicanism. That it might have been preserved in the Church of England of the twentieth century is another matter. It was not, and there is no way of making history turn back upon itself. The development of Methodism as a missionary movement which became a church is one of the great stories of modern Christianity.

CHAPTER TWO

METHODIST PREACHING

IN ADDITION to the attitudes, rules, and regulations which came over into the Methodist church from its origin as a religious society within the Church of England, there are also some things which we inherited from the nature of the century in which Methodism arose, from the frontier society in which Methodism flourished in America. Some of our inheritance has been a misunderstanding of the original Wesleyan evangel. Some of it has been in direct opposition to what Wesley himself believed and practiced.

For one thing, we have inherited an evangelistic tradition. The Methodist church is in its broadest sense a missionary movement, and from the start it was an evangelistic movement—although the word was not used in that day—going first to the lost sheep of the Church of England and then to the unchurched masses of the people. In the General Minutes the question is asked: "In what view may we and our helpers be considered?" The answer is: "Perhaps as extraordinary messengers, (that is, out of the ordinary way) designed, (1.) To provoke the regular Ministers to jealousy. (2.) To sup-

ply their lack of service toward those who are perishing
for want of knowledge." When Wesley spoke of pro-
voking the regular Ministers to jealousy he was using
an expression which stems from St. Paul's admonition to
provoke each other to godly works. The Methodist
preachers were to be considered as extraordinary messengers, out of the ordinary way of the church.

This extraordinary evangelistic mission of the Methodist preachers was limited in such a way that Wesley
did not believe a preacher could remain in one place
for any length of time. He declared that he himself
could not remain long. This probably was an exaggera-
tion, but it indicated Wesley's belief about the kind of
extraordinary preaching that the Methodist preacher
was sent out to do. Toward the end of his life, in May,
1784, he summed up his feelings about this matter:

In the evening I talked largely with the preachers, and
showed them the hurt it did both to them and the people
for any one preacher to stay six or eight weeks together in
one place. Neither can he find matter for preaching every
morning and evening, nor will the people come to hear him.
Hence he grows cold by lying in bed, and so do the people.
Whereas if he never stays more than a fortnight in one place
he may find matter enough, and the people will gladly hear
him.[1]

A preacher who preached twice every day and was
confined to evangelistic sermons obviously could not
remain very long in one place unless he were to beat old
straw. The way in which the Methodist preachers
offered variety to their congregations was not in that
they pursued other than evangelistic lines in their
preaching, but that the preachers themselves were
different. Forty years ago Corra Harris, in a book that
did not please some Southern Methodists, *A Circuit*

Rider's Widow, explained this as it applied nearly a
century and a half after Wesley's death:

> The only change of scenes I had for thirty years was just
> a change of pastors in our church. Every time a new
> preacher comes he brings a new setting for the same old
> gospel. One magnifies the glory of God, another His Infi-
> nite Mercies. One cries, "Repent! Repent, for the Kingdom
> of Heaven is at hand." Another founds his ministry upon
> this: "Come unto me, all ye that labour and are heavy laden,
> and I will give you rest." Now and then we get an old cross-
> grained Isaiah who preaches with the red-hot coals of fire
> from the bottomless pit and scares some of the worst sinners
> into the fold, literally smoking from their narrow escape.
> It all comes for the same thing. I never worry as some do
> about whether they can or cannot agree with what the
> pastor said in his morning sermon. I know by long experi-
> ence that all kinds of preachers are needed to win all the
> different kinds of sinners, and even then the sinners seem to
> increase faster than the saints.[2]

Wesley would be understood as to the matter of the
preaching which he wanted his helpers to follow.
He himself spent quite a lot of time upon what we
should now call ethical preaching, as his series dealing
with the Sermon on the Mount proves. The Methodists
were plagued with what was called "gospel preaching."
Wesley said that this preaching was entirely new to the
Methodists and defined it as "speaking much of the
promises, little of the commands."[3] He thought it had
done great harm. His directions as set forth in the
minutes are:

The most effectual way of preaching Christ, is to preach
Him in all his offices, and to declare His law as well as His
gospel, both to believers and unbelievers. Let us strongly
and closely insist upon inward and outward holiness, in all
its branches.[4]

If the Methodist preachers followed John Wesley's directions—and as a usual thing they did—they preached morning and night for about two weeks at a place. Then they moved on to another part of the work assigned to them. We have here something similar to the revival meetings that later became such a feature in American Methodist churches. But it was taken for granted, by Wesley at least, that these meetings did not fulfil all the demands of Christian worship. When Methodists objected that they did not like to hear the local Church of England clergymen preach, Wesley replied that they could get benefit in hearing practically every sermon preached from the Church of England pulpits. As we have noted, he felt that the prayers of the Methodist preachers should not be substituted for the prayers in the *Book of Common Prayer*. The Methodist preacher prayed extempore, and Wesley thought he ought not to pray more than three or four minutes at a time.

Here, then, is another of the anomalies of the Methodist church. It has inherited the evangelistic tradition of the Methodist Societies; but it has sometimes neglected the other tradition of the Methodist church which was that the evangelistic services were to be supplemented by church services.

But some may say, "Our own service is public worship." Yes; but not such as supersedes the Church service; it presupposes public prayer, like the sermons at the University. If it were designed to be instead of the Church service, it would be essentially defective; for it seldom has the four grand parts of public prayer, deprecation, petition, intercession, and thanksgiving.[5]

As people with other than a Church of England background joined the Societies, Wesley was willing that they should attend church services of their choice. But he preferred his own.

In order to perpetuate church services in America, Wesley abridged *The Book of Common Prayer* and transmitted it to the newly organized Methodist Episcopal church in this country. This abridgment was known as *The Sunday Service*. Bishop Nolan Harmon in his *The Rites and Ritual of Episcopal Methodism* (Publishing House of the M. E. Church, South, 1926) has a very helpful chapter on this book. The Christmas Conference of 1784 adopted *The Sunday Service* and apparently regarded it as a guide in their work. The phrase "According to our Liturgy" or "prescribed by our Liturgy" occurs in the Minutes and indicates that *The Sunday Service* was regarded as an integral part of the new Methodist church. Harmon is correct, as are the other classical commentators upon the Methodist *Rites and Ritual,* in observing that it was not in the nature of things for the new Methodist church in a new land to be a liturgical church. Bishop Harmon observes: "The *Book of Methodism,* instead of a *Prayer Book* became a discipline—not *ordered worship,* but ordered *life and activity.*"[6]

I think this is a very just observation. What the founder of Methodism would have thought, however, about a religious movement that was simply ordered life and activity and did not include ordered worship is something else.

Methodism has inherited the evangelistic tradition; but it has not kept, particularly in the United States, the full evangelistic tradition as the early Methodists understood it. In August, 1763, Wesley declared as a result of visiting several parts of the country where the Methodists had preached: "I was more convinced than ever that the preaching like an apostle, without joining together those that are awakened and training them up in the ways of God, is only begetting children for the murderer."[7]

At first societies were organized, and these were also grouped in "bands" on the model of the Moravian groups that John Wesley knew. These bands were continued, but it was found that they did not serve the needs of many of the Methodists. It is easy to understand why when one considers what was required of the band members. They were to be confronted, for example, with such inquiries as these: "What known sins have you committed since our last meetings? What temptations have you met with? How were you delivered? What have you thought, said, or done, of which you doubt whether it be sin or not? Have you nothing you desire to keep secret?"[8]

It is understandable that not too many Methodists were far enough advanced to be confronted constantly with questions of this sort. There were temperamental problems as well as simple problems of right and wrong. But the bands were a means of keeping some of the Methodists at a spiritual level that they perhaps could not have maintained otherwise.

The main instrument, however, by which the evangelistic work of the Methodist preacher was followed up and made more or less permanent was the class meeting. This became a part of Methodist organization in 1742, and, appropriately enough for Methodists, it came about as the result of consideration of a financial problem. At Bristol there was the question of trying to meet a debt. A sea captain suggested that the Society be broken up into smaller groups and that he would take eleven poorer members. If they could not each pay a penny a week he would pay it for them. So, the Society was organized into what Wesley called "classes."

Soon he found that he had obtained precisely what he wanted for the purpose of looking after his membership. The classes met every week. They might consist of six or seven members or more. Class leaders were under strict regulations and strict supervision. These men met with the classes usually in the evening, sometimes in the early morning before the members went to work, and only occasionally in the afternoons.

We begin to see here in outline some of the things that the Methodists did for the people to whom they brought their evangelistic message. It is perhaps not far-fetched to see an analogy between the workings of Alcoholics Anonymous and those of the early Methodists. I do not for a moment suppose that there has been any conscious imitation of the early Methodists in the methods of Alcoholics Anonymous. But this organization, which has had a more successful record than any I know in looking after alcoholics, has followed a method which is in many ways precisely what the early Methodists did. In so doing they have sometimes received rebukes from evangelistic preachers who still feel that the total sum of evangelism is in preaching a sermon. Actually the Methodists did not so learn their gospel, whatever may be true of other denominations.

Alcoholics Anonymous begins with the requirement that a man confess his inability to cope with his temptation. He has to be willing to say: "I am an alcoholic, and I cannot help myself." He has to come to the point where he believes that there must be help from some power outside himself. The likeness to the requirement of the early Methodist preacher that a man must confess his sins and admit his helplessness is evident.

But there are some other things which we need to notice. The early Methodist convert was not left to himself. He belonged to a group. This group met regularly. The early Methodist member had to meet with the Society; he had to meet with his class; he was supposed to attend the services of the church, if those services were available; and he was certainly supposed to attend the Methodist service when that Methodist service was held. As a matter of fact, there was not too much time left.

This is precisely what Wesley intended. He said somewhere that religion takes up just as much of your time as you have left over from trying to make a living. And when the Methodists went out into the highways and byways, appealing to men and women who had never heard of the Christian religion, or to those who had become decided in their sins, the convert was not left with some emotional experience as his only safeguard. He was not left with a vacuum that might be filled by his slipping back into his old ways. The Methodists furnished their members something to occupy their time as fully as was needed.

Again, the early Methodist was expected to become busy about the needs of other people. In the class meetings, and certainly in the band meetings, experiences were exchanged. Each was supposed to be able to help another. Moreover, the lay people were supposed to take an active part in the process of awakening men to their religious needs. They were supposed to keep busy with charitable works. There was no possibility that one could continue in the Methodist Societies without sufficient activity to take most of the spare time that anybody was likely to have.

All this was on the assumption that a man lives, as Wesley loved to put it, "moment by moment." He did not like to hear people talk about sanctified states or justified states. He thought that implied a plateau of spiritual experience which was not normal for human beings. He felt that life was a succession of moments, and that a man's spiritual experience was to be judged by the particular moment in which the matter was considered. It is true that a man's sins were forgiven, and that he might proceed in the development of his spiritual life; but it was not supposed that all of a man's strength would come to him at one time. Just as the alcoholic is encouraged by Alcoholics Anonymous to limit his determination to abstain from alcoholic drinks to a small period of time—a day, or even a part of a day—so the Methodist was to live moment by moment.

This, incidentally, has been the cause of some of the misunderstandings of people who have traditionally thought that the way to combat the individual's desire for alcohol is to have him "take the pledge." Taking a pledge for a lifetime or for a year is taking a pledge for too much time, according to those who have dealt with Alcoholics Anonymous. They think that man cannot so command his life as to look forward over a long period of months or years; but a man can take care of a few hours at a time. This is similar to the Methodists' method of taking care of their converts. And it is part of the secret of the Methodists' success with some of the worst characters of the eighteenth century.

The evangelism of early Methodism, then, was not simply the preaching of sermons and the response of people to an emotional appeal. The sermons were preached, and a high value was set upon such preaching. As we shall see, the scenes were truly emotional. But evangelism, to borrow the modern term, was not to the early Methodist a matter of "holding meetings." It was the preaching of the gospel followed up by these practical matters. A fellowship was created, as Leslie Church has so well pointed out, in which a man might find those

who were to help him with his problems. Continual
oversight was exercised in a cure of souls that was real
and practical. And the philosophy of the movement was
such that men were not expected to settle once for all
their life's destiny. They were expected moment by
moment to work out their salvation. It was true that
they believed in instantaneous conversion, but they also
believed in gradual conversion, and, more important,
they believed in constant reliance upon divine help
and upon those human conditions which they believed
a part of the process of salvation.

Along with this evangelistic inheritance which has
come down to the Methodists is the religion of the
heart. Frequently, using a term that was applied to a
Lutheran movement on the Continent, Methodism is
referred to as a "pietistic" religion. There is essential
truth in this description of the Methodist movement.
Like movements on the Continent and in England,
it tried to rescue religion from the belief in certain
doctrines, the observance of certain rites and rules, and
make it a religion which was the expression of man's
deepest affections. It is one thing to obey because obedience is required; it is another thing to obey because one
loves to obey. Anyone who knows something of the
"religious" debates that were a common spectacle in
this country a couple of generations ago, or who is
acquainted with the more sophisticated arguments that
go on endlessly now in certain religious groups about
doctrines and usages, will understand that eventually
people tire of these things. England had lived through a
period of turmoil during the seventeenth century, not
only a spiritual turmoil but one ending in a bloody civil
war. This turmoil had been preceded and accompanied
by endless discussions of fine points of doctrine. Also
preceding and accompanying this revolution were end-

less discussions about rites and ceremonies. It was only natural that the country should try to settle down and forget about fine points of doctrine—and, unfortunately, forget much about moral rules.

Recent psychological writers have given full credit to the emotions as a part of the life of man. In point of fact, it looks sometimes as if some of our psychologists do not believe that man has anything except emotions. But certainly the place of emotions in our ordinary life cannot be deprecated. And in the eighteenth century there was a strong movement toward the proper evaluation of emotion. It took the form of psychological theory; it appeared in the new literary form, the novel; it was apparent in the poetry of the day. Literary historians are fond of tracing the beginnings of what is called the Romantic movement. Certainly that movement began in the eighteenth century and moved swiftly toward the flowering of the early nineteenth century. It was fitting that the religious movement called Methodist should also lay great stress upon the emotions.

It would be well, however, to remember that the emotions of the Methodists were not always wild and uncontrolled. John Nelson, one of the greatest of Wesley's preachers, describes an experience that he had in Saint Paul's Cathedral:

About ten days before Christmas I went to Saint Paul's; and while I was at the communion-table, I felt such an awful sense of God resting upon me that my heart was like melting wax before Him; and all my prayer was, "Thy will be done! Thy will be done!" I was so dissolved into tears of love that I could scarce take the bread . . .[9]

Not all the emotional manifestations of the early Methodists, however, were just outpourings of a man's feelings as he knelt at the altar. There are still those who

remember when the appellation of the Methodists was
"the noisy Methodists." It is unnecessary to quote
accounts of the hysterical scenes which took place frequently in the early days of the Methodist movement
both in England and in America. Some dissertations
have been written on the subject, and there is no question as to the actuality of these scenes.

It is to be kept in mind that these outbreaks were not
encouraged by the Wesleys themselves. It is true that
John Wesley, in particular, shared many of the beliefs
of his time and was very careful not to pass judgment
upon outbreaks that he did not always understand; but
neither of the brothers encouraged these manifestations,
and they disappeared. The reason they disappeared
under Charles Wesley is very evident:

Saturday, June 4 (1743) [runs the entry in the *Journal*],
I went on at five expounding the Acts. Some stumbling-
blocks, with the help of God, I have removed, particularly
the fits. Many, no doubt, were, at our first preaching, struck
down, both soul and body into the depth of distress. Their
outward affections were easy to be imitated. Many counter-
feits I have already detected. To-day, one who came from
the alehouse, drunk, was pleased to fall into a fit for my
entertainment, and beat himself heartily. I thought it a pity
to hinder him; so, instead of singing over him, as had been
often done, we left him to recover at his leisure. Another,
a girl, as she began her cry, I ordered to be carried out.
Her convulsion was so violent, as to take away the use of her
limbs, till they had laid and left her without the door. Then
immediately she found her legs and walked off. Some very
unstill sisters, who always took care to stand near me, and
tried which should cry loudest, since I had them removed
out of my sight have been as quiet as lambs. The first night
I preached here half my words were lost through their
outcries. Last night before I began, I gave public notice
that whosoever cried so as to drown my voice should, without any man's hurting or judging them, be gently carried to

the farthest corner of the room. But my porters had no
employment the whole night; yet the Lord was with us
mightily convincing of sin and of righteousness.[10]

Methodism was an emotional religion so far as its
outward manifestations were concerned, partly because
it sprang from an emotional era. Those who have studied
the neoclassic literature of the early part of the eighteenth century are not always aware of the emotional
character of the people themselves. But as a matter of
fact when the Methodists talked about being of a
"sorrowful spirit" they were only talking the language
of the century. The fear of death was characteristic of
the eighteenth century as it was of the Middle Ages.
Perhaps the best-known poem of the eighteenth century
is Gray's "Elegy in a Country Churchyard." And the title
of that poem means nothing more than "A Dirge in a
Graveyard." One of its most familiar stanzas is:

> The boast of heraldry, the pomp of power,
>   And all that beauty or wealth e'er gave,
> Await alike the inevitable hour;
>   The paths of glory lead but to the grave.

Anyone who knows the literature of the mid–eighteenth century knows that it dripped with tears.

In Edward Eggleston's *The Circuit Rider* there is a
description of a Methodist service at a camp meeting in
early America. In some respects it would not be untrue
to the Methodists of England or of any other place:

He [the preacher] prayed as a man talking face to face
with the Almighty Judge of the generations of men; he
prayed with an undoubting assurance of his own acceptance
with God, and with the sincerest conviction of the intimate
peril of his unforgiven hearers. It is not argument that
reaches men but conviction; and for immediate practical

purposes, one Tishbite Elijah that can thunder out of a heart that never doubts, is worth a thousand cute writers of ingenious apologies.

When it comes, however, to a description of the sermon, it is necessary to keep in mind that one is talking about the preaching that in many ways was characteristic of the Methodists. Eggleston is speaking:

But the early Westerners were as inflammable as tow; they did not deliberate, they were swept into most of their decisions by contagious excitements. And never did any class of men understand the art of exciting by oratory more perfectly than the old western preachers. The simple hunters to whom they preached had the most absolute faith in the invisible. The Day of Judgment, the doom of the wicked, and the blessedness of the righteous were as real and substantial in their conception as any facts in life. They could abide no refinements. The terribleness of Indian warfare, the relentlessness of their own revengefulness, the sudden lynchings, the abandoned wickedness of the lawless, and the ruthlessness of mobs of "regulators" were a background upon which they founded the most materialistic conception of hell and the most literal understanding of the Day of Judgment.[11]

It is commonly taken for granted that the early Methodist preachers spent their time, as did the frontier preachers in this country, shaking men over the coals of hell fire and appealing to what Eggleston calls the most materalistic conception of the Day of Judgment. That the Wesleys themselves believed in future punishment there is no question. That the early Methodists sometimes preached in the tones which Eggleston describes there is also no question. But the predominant preaching is of another type.

For a proper understanding of the Wesleys themselves one must take into consideration the difference between Charles Wesley, the poet, and John Wesley, the preacher and organizer of Methodism. Actually, John Wesley himself, while intensely interested in the experiences of those people with whom he came into contact, was not a man of obvious emotion. I cannot do better than to quote words that I wrote over twenty years ago in a book now out of print:

Indeed, Wesley was by nature and training little fitted for experiences of emotional intensity. Throughout his life he had rationed his time and allotted his past with a methodicity impossible to more romantic natures. Sometimes, even in his old age, he looked back with a kind of nostalgia to the ordered days at Oxford. "Let me be again an Oxford Methodist!" He cried to Charles in 1772. "I am often in doubt whether it would not be best for me to resume all my Oxford rules, great and small. I did then walk closely with God and redeem the time." Feelings are desirable, but Wesley could not rid himself of his reliance upon reason administering by the rules of logic. In 1786, he wrote to Elizabeth Ritchie that he had not heard or read of anything like his own experience. Count Zinzendorf had said that there are three ways by which God leads his people: by apposite text of scripture, by impressions, by plain and clear reasons. Wesley had been led by reason and scripture, but rarely by impressions. "I see," he wrote, "abundantly more than I feel." And there is something pathetic in the line with which he concludes: "I want to feel more love and zeal for God."

"I want to feel"—this is a recurring note in Wesley's long years. Not that he was by any means devoid of feeling, but there was not that ebullience of emotion which some seem to have. The reader who comes to Wesley's *Journal* with the idea that he was a preacher of feeling cannot but be surprised at the paucity of references to the great evangelist's own feelings. There are occasional entries: "The longer I spoke the more strength I had, till at twelve I was as one refreshed with wine"; "I explained the nature of inward religion, words flowing upon me faster than I could speak"; "I intended to have given an exhortation to the Society, but as soon as we met, the Spirit of supplication fell upon us,

so that I could hardly do anything but pray and give thanks."
But compared to the mass of the *Journal* such entries are
rare. The high emotional experiences recorded there are of
other people. Wesley himself had earnests of the feeling
which others had, and he would have liked to feel more.
In the 1737 hymn book, he transcribed Addison's hymn,
"When all Thy Mercies, O My God," my rising soul surveys;
but the latter lines of the first stanza he changed to read

> Why my cold heart, art thou not lost
> In wonder, love and praise?

rather than, as originally,

> Transported with the view, I'm lost
> In wonder, love and praise.

It is illustrative of the ease with which theories can be made
that this, on first glance, seems only a proof of Wesley's pre-
converted state of soul. But Wesley never changed the line.
To the time of his last hymn book, he continued to reprint
the hymn as he had printed it almost half a century before.
Apparently, to the end it was to him a remarkable fact that
he felt no more than he did.[12]

John Wesley came honestly by his emotional stability.
A great many pages have been spent in praising Susannah Wesley for her influence upon her son John; but
frequently the writers do not take the trouble to find out
in just what ways the mother did influence the son.
A revealing light on one phase of this matter comes
from a letter which Mrs. Wesley wrote to John in 1727.
John had signed his last letter not as usually, "Your Dutiful Son," but "Your affectionate, dutiful Son." In writing
in answer to this letter his mother commented: "Dear
Son, the conclusion of your letter is very kind. That you
were ever dutiful, I very well know. But I know myself
enough to rest satisfied with a moderate degree of your
affection. Indeed it would be unjust in me to desire the
love of anyone."[13]

I have labored this point because of the widespread
notion that Methodism began in an emotional debauch,
which subsided only as the church became respectable.
This has been especially abetted by most people's ideas
of the American camp meeting. Charles A. Johnson's
The Frontier Camp Meeting: Religion's Harvest Time,
recently published by the Southern Methodist University Press, should help to give a scholarly and objective
picture of a much-abused phenomenon in frontier life.

There was not the overflow of unrestricted emotion in
early Methodism which is often pictured. But whatever
the case with *early* Methodism, there is obviously not
much danger that *modern* Methodism will be too
emotional. The average Methodist church today is a cool
and collected haven for unexcited Christians. This is
true, of course, because the times have changed. Only at
football games and election rallies do we any longer let
ourselves go. The ordinary life of men is purged emo-
tionally by endless debauches of sentiment in plays
and books. There are few tears left for religious crises.

We can agree, I think, that the values of habit and of
a disciplined life are apparent to most people today,
even if they only admire the better part. It is unfortunate
that such a name as "Methodist" should represent emotional excess. The name itself stands for discipline.
But we have unfortunately inherited—if only in memory
—a tradition of great emotion. Such are the ironies of
history.

But we should be losing greatly if we forget that early
Methodism was emotional.

What actually happened, at least in this country, is
that the practice of seeking the conversion of men, with
the accompanying requirements of repentance for sin,
has gone through three stages in our recent history.

In the first place, we ritualized our evangelistic efforts. There was a time not far back in our history when the whole process was as stylized as some modern paintings. There must be a revival meeting, with an "altar" and certain emotional songs sung at the right time. Many of these meetings were of great help. Great Britain still remembers with gratitude Dwight L. Moody, though many of those who still think of religion as the crossing of the t's and the dotting of the i's of some theological doctrines have never been able to understand the attraction of Moody for some English and Scottish intellectuals.

Our next step was to commercialize our evangelical appeals. The itinerant evangelist—or one should say some of them, for there were consecrated men among the number—would enter the local parish and stir up great excitement by attacking the church itself and everything that could be thought of. Then the evangelist would frequently collect more money than the pastor saw during the entire year and retire to other fields. Later the single evangelist became a team equal to a modern football coaching staff. There were line coaches and backfield coaches and the rest. The conversion of men became an expensive business.

Later we organized the process. Following (perhaps preceding in time) the organization for money-raising, the community was surveyed so that no lurking son of Satan might escape, and the work was on. Preferably it should be done in a day—or at least a week. There was not much time for soul-searching. The cards were ready, and the ink flowed freely.

I have not mentioned these stages in our progress or regress as a matter of ridicule. Under all of the systems good has been done. It was inevitable that the American passion for advertising and promotion should come

into our churches. There is a sense in which all evangelism is promotion. But the crux of the matter is
always: What is being promoted?

One cause for our distrust of worship and personal
feeling in religion is, of course, that we are a nation of
extroverts. Once to an academic audience I dared to
quote Kipling:

And the Sons of Mary smile and are blessèd — they know the
Angels are on their side.
They know in them is the Grace confessèd, and for them are
the Mercies multiplied.
They sit at the Feet — they hear the Word — they see how
truly the Promise runs.
They have cast their burden upon the Lord, and — the Lord
He lays it on Martha's Sons!

Indeed, Kipling is so sure that the Lord of Heaven
and Earth could never have endorsed the conduct of
Mary in leaving her sister to prepare a meal while she
sat at the Master's feet, that he invented a reason:

And because she lost her temper once, and because she was
rude to the Lord her Guest,
Her Sons must wait upon Mary's Sons, world without end,
reprieve, or rest.

The real secret is work. The proper activity of man
is planning for the future—sometimes a very far and
hazy future. For a man to talk about joy and peace and
hope springing from simple trust is a little out of place.
It is true that we have ulcers and high blood pressure.
It is true that one of our leading humorists has written a
book called *The Road to Miltown*. But there are three
conferences set up for tomorrow, and there may be time
for nine holes of golf at the end of the day.

Let us, then, be up and doing,
With a heart for any fate;

> Still achieving, still pursuing,
> Learn to labour . . .

But our world is disorganized. Not only societies but individuals are falling to pieces. That life can be orientated around a dominant affection is well enough known. The end cannot be achieved by little rules or by insistence upon declaring our belief in this or that side issue about which we probably know very little anyway.

Perhaps there is still a place for the United Societies with their "one only" rule for admission and for a gospel which is in essence the love of God and the love of man.

CHAPTER THREE

WHAT IS SALVATION?

WHAT DID the Wesleys preach? What was their "gospel"? Before considering this question one might well glance at the times and at the people to whom the Methodists appealed. There are certain resemblances to our own day that may help us to understand the Methodist message.

Usually it is thought enough if we emphasize the world disorder of eighteenth-century England. But other characteristics of the times should be noted.

This is not the first century in which men have found themselves moving as in a strange land. There have been other times when social conditions have changed, when the economy of a country has shifted, when the intellectual life of the people has taken some new turn. When I was a boy I was taught that Western history was divided into three parts: ancient, medieval, and modern. You could tie up these periods into neat packages, wrap them with ribbon of the appropriate color, and put them on the shelves confident that they would never interfere with each other. We know better now. The men of 1493 were not different from the men of 1491, although

Christopher Columbus had made an interesting discovery in the year between.

What makes the eighteenth century of interest, particularly for English-speaking people, is that the Middle Ages continued into that century—and for that matter beyond. But, on the whole, the eighteenth century was the transition century. The Middle Ages were dying, and the modern world was coming to birth.

At the beginning of the century in which Wesley was born, and in which he worked, most Englishmen lived in isolated villages or on lonely farms cut off from their fellows by trails that were frequently impassable. The economy was agricultural. By the end of the century many men and women—and unfortunately children, also —were making their living by working in factories. England was still an agricultural seafaring nation, but there were new ways to make a living; and people who had never had more than a bare subsistence could sometimes make more money than they had ever dreamed of making. Of course, others only starved in the cities instead of starving in the country. But the economy was changing.

Something else was happening: the old social order was breaking up. Money eventually does that to any social order. If people who have been on the bottom rung of the ladder begin to make money there is going to be a shift on the ladder. For one thing, people will go where there is a chance to make more. In eighteenth-century England people left the farms, partly because the old common fields were enclosed by the big landowners, but also because there was more money in town. Moreover, there were stirring in the air certain ideas which were doing a good deal to help break up the old social system.

Across the ocean some colonists of Great Britain had

gotten together and issued one of the most inflammatory documents of all time—a document which we hope is yet lighting fires in men's hearts. This document said: "We hold these truths to be self-evident, that all men are created equal, that they are endowed by their Creator with certain unalienable rights, that among these are life, liberty, and the pursuit of happiness." And the frightening thing was that it went on to say: "We hold ... that whenever any form of government becomes destructive of these ends, it is the right of the people to alter or abolish it ..."

The Americans went so far as to declare their independence and secure it in what we call the War of the Revolution. Wesley did not live to see the terror of the French Revolution, nor the Napoleonic dictatorship which followed, as dictatorships usually follow revolutions.

The century to which Methodism came also saw the British Isles under almost continuous fear of war. War was actually waged part of the time, but the fear was greater than the fact. The great enemy was France —France the Catholic power during the greater part of the century, and France the Republican terror in the last decade. But throughout the century there was also the fear not only of Catholics without but of treason within.

It is true that there was a rebellion in 1715 and again in 1745, but the event proved that few Englishmen were not true to their government. Englishmen who suspected their Catholic fellow-countrymen learned that most of them would have nothing to do with foreign intrigues. But when a country suspects that there are traitors in its midst, there is little place for reason.

One thing we must remember, and usually do not remember, is that an established order, just or unjust, is usually a very comfortable order to those who have accommodated themselves to it. This is not to defend injustice; it is simply to remark that when people are used to a certain order of life it is a wrench for them to change it.

As we look back on it now it does not seem that the English lost all of their class feeling in the eighteenth century; but as a matter of fact the old medieval order did crack, and there was much uneasiness on that account. Susannah Wesley used to speak of "the principle of subordination." By this she did not mean merely that children should obey their parents, but also that there was a place for everybody in the social structure, and that people should know their place. It was not quite what was meant by the satirical verse: "God bless the squire and his rich relations, and teach us all our proper stations." Nevertheless, Susannah did believe in an ordered world, and a world ordered as she had known it in the past.

When such a world begins to break up, two things always happen: those who have been on the bottom of the ladder, some of them at least, become cocksure and arrogant; and those on the top rungs of the ladder become uneasy and afraid. Consequently, any period in which the older order of society breaks becomes a hesitant and a fearful time.

Perhaps it should be noted, also, that the eighteenth century, in common with much of the Middle Ages, was obsessed by the idea of death. The great Isaac Watts, who could write the noble lines,

> I'll praise my Maker while I've breath,
> And when my voice is lost in death,
> Praise shall employ my nobler powers;
> My days of praise shall ne'er be past,

> While life, and thought, and being last,
> Or immortality endures.

was also the author of another hymn which appeared
for many years in the *Methodist Hymn Book:*

> Hark! From the tombs a doleful sound,
> My ears attend the cry:
> "Ye living men, come view the ground
> Where you must shortly lie."

As we have seen, the Methodists inherited part of
their sorrowful spirit from the mood of the times. Some
of the hymns also reflect that mood and the horror of
the eighteenth-century attitude toward death:

> Death rides on every passing breeze,
> And lurks in every flower;
> Each season has its own disease,
> Its peril every hour.

> Turn, mortal, turn! Thy danger know:
> Where'er thy foot can tread
> The Earth rings hollow from below,
> And warns thee of her dead!

In a time and a land where new economic forces were
changing the ways of life, and where the old accustomed
social order was breaking down with new cries about
liberty and the rights of men, yet where the old misery
and the fear of death bore heavily on men, what sort of
message did the new religious movement bring? It is
customary to begin the answer to this in theological
terms. One of the difficulties of all professions is that
the jargon of that profession, familiar enough to its
devotees, is too frequently used in an attempt to explain
what it means. Yet in a popular movement it should be
clear that no theological arguments would appeal to the

great masses of the people, many of whom were illiterate and most of whom had no theological background, and many of them no religious background at all. It is fortunate for us that the Wesleys had a habit of writing in plain and simple language and of speaking in the same way. It is true that when Wesley became theological he fell back upon terms which can be understood only in the light of theological history and of his century. But he did say enough so that we can understand how his message was spoken to the common people in such a way that they heard him gladly.

What, then, is the salvation that he preached to these people? In his great sermon, "The Scripture Way of Salvation," which was first published in 1765, he seems to have taken great care to put down carefully what he meant by his terms:

And, first, let us inquire, What is salvation? The salvation which is here spoken of is not what is frequently understood by that word, the going to Heaven, eternal happiness. It is not the soul's going to Paradise, termed by our Lord "Abraham's Bosom." It is not a blessing which lies on the other side death; or, as we usually speak, in the other world.

He goes on to explain that what he means by salvation is the entire work of God during man's lifetime. In his pamphlet, *An Earnest Appeal to Men of Reason and Religion,* he defines religion in this fashion:

And this we conceive to be no other than love; the love of God, and of all mankind; the loving God with all our heart and soul, and strength, as having first loved us, as the fountain of all the good we have received, and of all we ever hope to enjoy; and the loving every soul which God hath made, every man on earth, as our own soul.

In this pamphlet he explains that he considers this

love to be the medicine of life, and that wherever it is
there are "virtue and happiness, going hand in hand.
There is humbleness of mind, gentleness, long-suffering,
the whole image of God, and at the same time a peace
that passeth all understanding, and joy unspeakable and
full of glory."

To illustrate further what he meant, John Wesley fell
back on lines from his father's friend, Alexander Pope:

> Eternal sunshine of the spotless mind;
> Each pray'r accepted, and each wish resign'd:
> Desires composed, affections ever even,
> Tears of delight, and sighs that waft to Heav'n.

This note of peace and assurance was one of the marks
of early Methodism. John Haime, a soldier who fought
at Dettingen and Fontenoy and was one of Wesley's
traveling companions for a time, prayed when he was
dying at the age of eighty: "Grant us continually sweet
peace, quietness and the assurance of Thy favour."[1]

I realize that this is to open early Methodism to the
charge that it was devoted to "peace of mind." It was
actually so; but one must distinguish between the peace
of mind that consists in trying to remove all worries and
all concern and the peace of mind that rests upon a great
confidence that one can endure by the Grace of God.

Perhaps the best illustration of the nature of the peace
and confidence that was the heart of the Methodist
preaching about present salvation is to be found in
Wesley's own experience. Few events in modern Protestant history have been debated more than the nature of
Wesley's conversion on May 24, 1738. Dr. J. E. Rattenbury, one of the best of living Methodist historians, has
divided the interpretations into an evangelical conversion, a Catholic conversion (which he attributes
rightly to Father Piette), and a humanist interpretation

of Wesley's conversion. The latter interpretation he attributes (wrongly, I think) to me.[2]

To understand what happened to John Wesley in 1738 and to understand the nature of the Methodist message of salvation which was preached by Wesley and his followers until his death a half-century later, it is well to see just what he sought at that crucial time.

On the journey to America in 1735, when Wesley went as a representative of the Society for the Propagation of the Gospel, a severe storm arose. It is difficult for those whose experience of ocean storms is confined to the great ships on which most travelers sail, to understand just what severe storms meant in the little sailing vessels such as the one on which Wesley made that crossing. On board the ship were a number of Moravians, Germans emigrating to the new colony of Georgia. When the first storm had quieted down— a storm in which Wesley had said to himself, "How is it that thou hast no faith?" since he was unwilling to die and was ashamed of his fear—Wesley went to see about the Germans.

At seven I went to the Germans. I had long before observed the great seriousness of their behaviour. Of their humility they had given a continual proof, by performing those servile offices for the other passengers which none of the English would undertake; for which they desired and would receive no pay, saying, "It was good for their proud hearts," and "their loving Saviour had done more for them." And every day had given them occasion of showing a meekness which no injury could move. If they were pushed, struck, or thrown down, they rose again and went away; but no complaint was found in their mouth. There was now an opportunity of trying whether they were delivered from the spirit of fear, as well as from that of pride, anger, and revenge. In the midst of the psalm wherewith their service began, wherein we were mentioning the power of God, the

sea broke over, split the main sail in pieces, covered the ship,
and poured in between the decks, as if the great deep had
already swallowed us up. A terrible screaming began among
the English. The Germans looked up and without inter-
mission calmly sang on. I asked one of them afterward,
"Was you not afraid?" He answered, "I thank God, no."
I asked, "But were not your women and children afraid?"
He replied mildly, "No; our women and children are not
afraid to die."[3]

That this impressed Wesley is evident from the words
with which he closed his *Journal* entry for that day,
January 25, 1736: "This was the most glorious day
which I have hitherto seen."

What did the Moravians contribute to Methodism?
Certainly they did not teach John Wesley the doctrine
of justification by faith. It would be absurd to say of a
man of the broad reading and general knowledge that
John Wesley had, that he had never before heard of
justification by faith. All his subsequent life he believed
that he had learned the doctrine, as a doctrine, from
the Articles and homilies of the Church of England.
But there is no manner of doubt that the Moravians
contributed to his Christian experience and to his understanding of the way in which the experience that corre-
sponded to the doctrine of justification by faith fitted
into the Christian life. That he was expecting more
than he received on May 24, 1738, is important, but,
for the moment, beside the point.

When he was in Germany in 1738 (after his "conversion"), Wesley set down what he had heard from Peter
Boehler. He was near enough to the event so that he
should have remembered, and what he remembered
that Moravian friend to have taught was:

1. When a man has a living faith in Christ, then is he
   justified:

2. This is always given in a moment;
3. And in that moment he has peace with God;
4. Which he cannot have without knowing that he has it:
5. And being born of God he sinneth not:
6. Which deliverance from sin he cannot have without knowing that he has it.

For the record, it should be said that later Wesley decided a man can be saved without assurance, that is knowing that he is saved; that he that is born of God may commit sin. But for the moment this is what Peter Boehler taught, and this is apparently what Wesley was seeking.

In Germany Wesley met one Arvid Gradin, who gave him a definition of "the full assurance of faith." This was: "Repose in the blood of Christ, a firm confidence (*firma fiducia*) in God, and persuasion of his favour; the highest tranquility, serenity, and peace of mind, with a deliverance from every desire, and a cessation of all, even inward sin."

Gradin added, as his own experience, "in a word, my heart, which before was tossed like a troubled sea, was still and quiet and in a sweet calm."[4] This, said Wesley, "was the first account I ever heard from any living man of what I had before learned myself from the oracles of God, and had been praying for, (with the little company of my friends,) and expecting for several years."[5]

The truth is that as early as 1725 Wesley had written to his mother concerning the teaching of Jeremy Taylor. In this letter he said he agreed with Taylor that we can never be so certain of the pardon of our sins "as to be assured they will never rise up against us." But he added: "I am persuaded we may know if we are *now* in a state of salvation, since that is expressly promised in the holy scriptures to our sincere endeavors, and we are surely able to judge of our own sincerity."[6]

It is perfectly true that Wesley is mixing up here what in later years he distinguished. The point I am making is not his confusion of his doctrine of Christian perfection and his general doctrine of salvation, but the essential element in the experience of May 24, 1738: that Wesley became convinced that God had actually forgiven *his* sins. Later he was to make all sorts of distinctions about the witness of the Holy Spirit and the witness of our own spirit, and he was to decide that assurance was not necessary for salvation, particularly final salvation; but the freedom from uneasiness of mind and anguish of spirit that came through his experience in 1738 is something to be credited partly to the Moravians.

With it clearly in mind that Wesley had been taught by Boehler that assurance of forgiveness and of freedom from sin were the results of justifying faith, and that he had himself said that Arvid Gradin had been the first person he ever knew who had put into words what he had been seeking, let us look at the conversion experience itself.

The account is well known. After reading the New Testament at five o'clock in the morning Wesley attended an early service at Saint Paul's Cathedral. The anthem, "Out of the Deep Have I Called unto Thee, O Lord," had considerable effect upon him. In the evening he went to a society in Aldersgate Street where one was reading Luther's preface to the *Epistle to the Romans*.

About a quarter before nine, while he was describing the change which God works in the heart through faith in Christ, I felt my heart strangely warmed. I felt I did trust in Christ, Christ alone for salvation; and an assurance was given me that he had taken away *my* sins, even *mine*, and saved *me* from the law of sin and death.

It is to be noted that Wesley's experience is of salvation now. He has been forgiven of past sins; but he has a heart strangely warmed with the confidence of present salvation.

For some time it has been the habit of historians of Methodism to assume that anyone who does not interpret this experience as the climax of Wesley's religious life or as a conversion from sin to salvation or from Catholicism to Protestantism, has been following Piette. It is interesting that a common-sense interpretation of Wesley's experience, true to the facts, was made fifty years before Piette's book.

The official historian of the Moravian church, J. E. Hutton, has set down an account of Wesley's own experience which, I think, should be preserved:

As John Wesley returned to England from his three years' stay in America, he found himself in a sorrowful state of mind. He had gone with all the ardor of youth; he returned a spiritual bankrupt. On this subject the historians have differed. According to High-Church Anglicans, John Wesley was a Christian saint before he ever set eyes on Boehler's face; according to Methodists he had only a legal religion and was lacking in genuine saving faith in Christ. His own evidence on the question seems conflicting. At the time he was sure he was not yet converted; in later years he inclined to think he was. At the time he sadly wrote in his Journal, "I who went to America to convert others was never myself converted to God"; and then, years later, he added the footnote, "I am not sure of this." It is easy, however, to explain this contradiction. The question turns on the meaning of the word "converted." If a man is truly converted to God when his heart throbs with love for his fellows, with a zeal for souls, and with a desire to do God's holy will, then John Wesley, when he returned from America, was just as truly a "converted" man as ever he was in later life. He was devout in prayer; he loved the scriptures; he longed to be holy; he was pure in thought, in deed, and in speech; he was

self-denying; he had fed his soul on the noble teaching of
Law's "Serious Call"; and thus, in many ways, he was a
beautiful model of what a Christian should be, and yet,
after all, he lacked one thing which Peter Boehler possessed.
If John Wesley was converted then he did not know it
himself. He had no firm, unflinching trust in God. He was
not sure that his sins were forgiven. He lacked what Methodists call "assurance," and what Saint Paul called "Peace
with God." He had the faith, to use his own distinction, not
of a son, but only of a servant. He was good but he was not
happy; he feared God, but he did not dare to love Him;
he had not yet attained the conviction that he himself had
been redeemed by Christ; and if this conviction is essential
to conversion then John Wesley, before he met Boehler, was
not yet a converted man.[7]

Hutton's account is, I believe, correct. The contribution of the Moravians and Peter Boehler was in convincing Wesley that the assurance that I have confidence in
God through Christ, and that He loves *me* and that *my*
sins are forgiven, was of the greatest importance not
only to Wesley's personal life but to his missionary
effort. This personal experience was a great discovery
for Wesley, and he owed it to the Moravians.

Even then Wesley was astonished that he did not
find the transports of joy which he had thought would
accompany this kind of experience; and there were
other times when he was not at all sure about this
matter of transports of joy. But the point to be observed is that Peter Boehler had taught there were
two fruits inseparably attending true faith in Christ:
"Dominion over sin and constant peace from a sense of
forgiveness."

It was this constant peace which Wesley did not
receive on May 24, 1738, or apparently at any other
time. In practical fact he was not of the temperament
to be moved by any experience to the point where he

was constantly and consistently of the same temper. It is very easy to share Rattenbury's feelings when one realizes how Wesley "analyzes, defines, divides, subdivides, and must have often been worried by his own introspection" to the point where one can very well say, "when I read his syllogisms, dilemmas, trilemmas, and the like, I could sometimes wish that he had stuck to Greek at Oxford and never taken to Logic."[8]

The only legitimate criticism of Methodists' interpretations of Wesley's conversion is that they have sometimes made it the be-all and end-all of the Methodist movement. It was of tremendous importance, although I cannot agree that it was a conversion from Catholicism to Protestantism. It was the realization by the Wesleys of the actual power of faith conceived not as a doctrine nor as a belief in doctrines, but as the actual surrender of one's self. Along with this surrender of one's self went very naturally the conviction that the pardoning love of God was individual for one's self and something whose realization was powerful in one's life. It is this conviction that he has loved *me* and saved *me* that was the essence of the Aldersgate experience; it is this conviction and its importance for present salvation that is the essence of the Methodist preaching of justification by faith.

It is a little difficult to reconcile Wesley's statements. One must accept the fact that he sometimes made statements which on later consideration he had to modify. This is because he had a profound respect for experience. Believing as he did that experience is one criterion by which doctrines are to be checked, Wesley allowed himself at later times to correct statements that were obviously too broad. It is extremely difficult to explain how Wesley reconciles his statement that he was preaching the love of God and man before he had preached a new salvation by faith with the statement that he would have had to be saved on account of invincible ignorance—presumably during the period when he was preaching the doctrine for which he so strongly contended as the essential part of his faith—unless Wesley had come to find what, if it will not be regarded as a sacrilegious expression, one might call a short cut to present salvation.

The point is that the great contribution of the Moravians to Wesley was in their insistence upon the experience of present salvation which would come in a moment. Wesley later came to understand that it did not always come in a moment, although he contended for the possibility and for the fact of its having arrived in a moment in many instances.

It has become fashionable in recent years to derive the theology of the Wesley movement from Charles Wesley's hymns. Granting that some of them were written by John, and many of them approved by him, one must yet keep in mind that the poet—and Charles Wesley was a poet—fastens upon those aspects of his subject which have emotional depth and color. For this reason the hymns must be used with caution in trying to express niceties of doctrine. Nevertheless, they do represent the emotional tone, and for that matter they represent rather faithfully the preaching of the Wesley brothers. For this reason it is appropriate to notice how many of the hymns for those, for example, who are seeking redemption, stress this matter of redemption now.

> Come ye weary sinners, come,
>   All who groan to bear your load,
> Jesus calls his wanderers home:
>   Hasten to your pardoning God:
>   . . . .

> Now the promised rest bestow,
>   Rest from servitude severe,
> Rest from all our toil and woe,
>   Rest from all our grief and fear.
>
>   . . . .
>
> Lo! We come to Thee for ease,
>   True and gracious as Thou art,
> Now our groaning soul release,
>   Write forgiveness on our heart.

There was a peculiar fitness in the preaching of this message of salvation to eighteenth-century England. Many of the people to whom the message was preached were in new industrial districts where the church had made little provision. Many of them were literally unchurched people, although many were of course members of the established church and later of dissenting groups; but instead of coming to them with a message that by long toil men might attain to the perfection that William Law explained in his *Serious Call to a Devout and Holy Life,* the Wesleys and their followers came with a message of salvation now. The salvation that they were talking about was the salvation of the soul at the present time. Its first release was from a burden of sin, and its second gifts were the gifts of the Spirit, peace and joy and love.

The notion, therefore, that peace of mind is not something that the Christian can truly strive for, is certainly not Methodist. It is true that many of the efforts for peace of mind, which consist of evading the actual issues of life or of trying to meet these issues by substitutes for courage and honesty and righteous living, are bad enough. Certainly the obsession of many people with the desire that no trouble should worry them has led to an emphasis upon what we have called "adjustment," which is certainly not spiritually healthy. But the attitude of the early Methodists reflected in the Wesleyan

sermons and hymns, that those who had confidence in
God that through Jesus Christ he had looked with pardoning mercy upon the sinner and had shed abroad in
his heart the gifts of the Spirit, is healthful enough.
The gifts of the Spirit, peace and joy, were not the peace
and joy to be obtained from a neglect of the actualities
of life, but rather, as Wesley put it, from the conquering
power that they found in their faith.

We have been talking about something which Wesley
called present salvation, but present salvation raises
the question of final salvation. Here Wesley required
some additional consideration of his question.

With an intense conviction that "without holiness no man
can see the Lord," Wesley could not exclude inward and
outward holiness from the conditions of salvation, in the
ordinary sense of the word. But he was equally convinced
that present salvation, salvation from doubt and fear and
from guilt and sin, is by faith, although a faith with
conditions. Reconciliation of the two Wesley found in a
distinction between salvation as a present experience and
salvation as the final acceptance of man by God. In 1741
he read Bishop Bull's *Harmonica Apostolica*, in which the
distinction is made. At first Wesley was repelled by the idea,
but he was soon using it himself. In 1741, he was writing
that justification at the last day is on the condition of "both
inward and outward holiness." He thought that this ought
to meet the desires of all "who have hitherto opposed justification by faith alone merely upon a principle of conscience,
because he was zealous for holiness and good works."[9]

So far as he knew, all Christians believed that without
holiness no man can see the Lord. He thought that the
Roman doctrine of purgatory was introduced for this
reason. And he admitted that many believed that holiness is obtained only "in the article of death." He himself admitted that usually men are made holy only in

the article of death, but he thought there was hope that one could have holiness in this life. At any rate, holiness one must have. And this introduced the whole question of good works.

This is not the place to consider the theological problem involved, nor is it the place to consider Wesley's attempted resolution of his conflict. It is enough to point out that Wesley, a solid, eighteenth-century Briton, could not quite reconcile himself to some of the metaphysical speculations concerning his subject. Common sense, as he understood it, told him that a man must do good. He believed unswervingly in the doctrine of justification by faith. How he worked out these two problems is another matter.

At present it is necessary to point out that when Wesley talks about salvation he is talking about two different kinds of salvation: present and final. For present salvation a man must have a sure trust and confidence. For final salvation there must be holiness of life achieved by faith during man's lifetime or in the hour and article of death—but holiness there must be.

What did the preaching of salvation so interpreted mean for England? It has been asserted that Methodism was simply an opiate for the people, that it prevented a French Revolution in Britain by fastening the minds of people on the joys of the next world. Only a complete misunderstanding of the nature of the Methodist message could justify any such interpretation.

The Wesleys believed devoutly in the existence of what we call the next world; they preached the reality of it; they believed in future rewards and punishment (literal punishment). But their gospel was to deliver men and women from the fear of that other world, and, thus, to give peace and joy in this world. True, they did not believe that this peace and joy could be had without effort or without trust in God through Jesus Christ. But they gave to their hearers an invitation to a peaceful and happy life. And if they came to realize how few, like Arvid Gradin, attained to that sweet calm of spirit in this life, still they held to their ideal. And they preached salvation now.

CHAPTER FOUR

DO METHODISTS HAVE A THEOLOGY?

AN ANGLICAN WRITER discussing certain seventeenth-century divines spoke some apposite words to people of his own communion. He said that a wide knowledge in theology, ranging from patristics to modern exponents of Continental confessional theology, is desirable. Moreover, he sees no danger in grafting such study on "existing theological stock." The danger arises when one makes alien theologies the background. "There follows a loss of root and idiom, and by neglecting these specifically Anglican presuppositions, latent or expressed in classical Anglican thought and writings, we risk becoming mere theological vagantes."[1]

The danger to which Methodism has too frequently succumbed lies in embracing theologies foreign to her basic assumptions and in accepting these as background. It is for this reason largely that we have seemed to many to have been wanderers on the face of the theological world.

Recent statements from English Methodist scholars have pointed to the problem. R. Kissack, for example, writing in *London Quarterly and Holborn Review*, April,

1956, criticizes statements issued by the British Methodist Conference. These statements, put forth in 1937 and 1939, are written, contends Kissack, "as if Methodism had emerged straight from the Continental Reformation, or from British Dissent."

Another British Methodist, Dr. C. A. Bowmer, author of the best work on Wesley's doctrine of the Last Supper, says bluntly:

Methodism can simply claim its place in the Holy Catholic Church which is the Body of Christ. It lies in the main stream of orthodox developments. Its roots are firmly embedded in the historical facts of the Christian faith. Methodists are not Dissenters.[2]

These statements will not mean as much to Americans as they doubtless mean to their British readers. Before discussing the general nature of Methodist theology, it might be wise for us to say a few words about the understanding of Wesley. He has been interpreted as a reviewer of Catholic doctrine, as a man who restated the essential Reformation doctrines, as a herald of the so-called liberalism of the nineteenth century, as all things to all men.

In connection with Wesley's theology, another preliminary statement should be made: John Wesley lived a long time. This is a commonplace observation, but Methodist historians do not always remember it. One of the best books on John Wesley's theology slips at this very point—neglect of a critical, historical study of his writings. The story will illustrate the necessity for remembering that Wesley lived long enough to change his mind.

Wesley is quoted as severely criticizing one of the worthies of the previous generation, Bishop George Bull. Wesley did criticize him, but what escaped the historian's attention was that the day Wesley wrote his criticism in his *Journal* was the day that he began reading the Bishop's book, *Harmonica Apostolica.* According to Wesley's Diary he was reading the book for several days afterward. Four years later Wesley was using Bishop Bull's argument. Thirty years later, Wesley said frankly: "It is true thirty years ago I was very angry with Bishop Bull, that great light of the Christian Church, because in his *Harmonica Apostolica* he distinguished between our first and second Justification."[3] But by this time Bull's distinction had become part of Wesley's own theological framework.

This simply means that Wesley reviewed and sometimes corrected former positions in the light of his own experience and knowledge or in consideration of the experiences and statements of others. The student of Wesley, therefore, must not remain satisfied with isolated sentences. His theology must be learned by a study of his total experience and beliefs.

John Wesley was a son of the English church with all its compromises and comprehensions. But he was a son of one branch of that church. Dr. Rattenbury says somewhere that we inherit ideas and attitudes from our parents and not from our grandparents. This was certainly true in eighteenth-century England; both of Wesley's grandfathers had been ejected at the Restoration, but his parents had read themselves back into the Established Church. Like most converts, they held their beliefs all the more tenaciously. Both of them belonged to the High Church wing.

A look at what this High Church inheritance meant will help to make Wesley's theological inheritance clearer. In worship Wesley inherited a predilection for what we would call Anglo-Catholic devotion. It is estimated that during his evangelical ministry John Wesley partook of the Lord's Supper on an average of once every four or five days. Apparently his ideas about the significance of the Lord's Supper did not change.

His ideas about the ordinance of Baptism are not entirely clear. In later life he reprinted his father's tract on Baptism without any indication that the doctrine of baptismal regeneration was not acceptable. But when he prepared the Sunday Services for the use of the Americans he did make changes that would seem to show a dislike for that doctrine.

Some of his High Church views he did change. His wider experience modified his attitude toward Dissenters. A few years after his experience at Aldersgate Wesley decided that episcopal ordination at the hands of a bishop possessing the Apostolic Succession was not necessary to a valid ministry or a valid administration of the sacraments.

Another inheritance from his High Church background was a reverence for the pre-Augustinian church. He did not regard the Fathers as equal in authority with Scripture, but he did think them "the most authentic commentators on Scripture, as being both nearest the fountain, and eminently imbued with that Spirit by whom all Scriptures was given." He added that it would be easily perceived that he referred to those who wrote before the Council of Nicaea. "But who would not likewise desire," he continued, "to have some acquaintance with those that followed them? With St. Chrysostom, Basil, Jerome, Austin [that is, Augustine], and above all, the man of a broken heart, Ephraim Syrus?"[4]

There is theological significance to this preference of the Fathers before 325 A.D. So far as is known there is no formulation of the doctrine of predestination before Augustine (354-430). Rejection of the doctrine of election is, therefore, natural enough for those who honored

Augustine but did not include him among those who were "the most authentic commentators on Scripture."

On January 24, 1738, when Wesley was returning from America, he set down an account of his scriptural condition in the light of his history. He recognized that he had made some serious errors. Among them was the fact that he had regarded antiquity as "a co-ordinate rather than subordinate rule with Scripture." Another error he had made was in extending the ancient period too far, "even to the middle or end of the fourth century."[5]

Since the High-Churchmen of the seventeenth and early eighteenth centuries had great reverence for the early church, some of them did not like to be called Arminians. Cosin, Thorndike, and Bull, although opposed to the doctrine of predestination, would not call themselves Arminians.[6] For later times the word has become associated with the activities of Archbishop Laud. As Norman Sykes put it: "It is unfortunate that the epithet of 'Laudian' has become inseparably associated with the Arminian tradition in England; for Laud has had an unusually bad press."[7]

As a matter of fact, it was not uncommon in the early part of the century to link together Arminianism and Popery. This could be one of the reasons for that peculiar accusation brought a number of times against the Methodists, that they were Papists in disguise. It is not of importance here whether Laud has been justly or unjustly condemned. There is a tendency now to regard him as the champion of liberty against those who opposed his theological positions.[8] But whether or not this be true, it is certainly true that the Methodists did inherit through Wesley the tradition of Arminian theology.

The word *Arminianism* came from Arminius (1560-

1609), the Dutch theologian who, called upon to defend Calvin's doctrines, found himself sympathizing with Calvin's critics. It has been said that Wesley returned more nearly to the original doctrine of Arminius than many of his predecessors. At any rate, it should be remembered that the Arminianism which Wesley inherited was in many ways a home-grown product. When Grotius came to England and spoke to others about the Arminian position he found that much about which he was talking was advocated already by Englishmen. As McAdoo says about the Caroline Divines, "If everything was grist to their mill, the mill was a home-product."[9]

Arminianism is not the doctrine that man can save himself. There is a tendency now to speak as if any theory not Calvinistic in its essence is a doctrine of free will on man's part, meaning that man has naturally the power to perform such actions as will make him acceptable in the sight of God. This is Pelagianism, not Arminianism. Arminianism held to conditional predestination.

Wesley called himself an Arminian. His magazine was named the *Arminian Magazine*. That he inherited the doctrine of "Free Grace" is beyond question. Both his father and his mother were agreed in opposing predestination. Samuel Wesley expressed his views in verse:

> None are excluded from the proffer'd Grace,
> It reaches all of Abraham's faithful Race;
> To Children and the Gentile World extends,
> And only with the Line of Nature ends.[10]

Susannah expressed herself in more positive terms. In 1725, John wrote his mother concerning some statements of Thomas à Kempis which had disturbed him.

She replied that she did not know Thomas à Kempis, but if John had quoted him correctly, she thought him "extremely in the wrong in that impious, I was about to say blasphemous suggestion, that God, by an irrevocable decree, has determined any man to be miserable even in this world."[11]

In all this Samuel and Susannah were simply agreeing with that High Church theology which they had adopted after their own independent study. Whether they liked the term Arminian or preferred to believe that they held simply to the doctrine of the pre-Augustinian church, the High-Churchmen of the seventeenth century generally agreed with John Bramhall, that "none are excluded from the benefits of Christ's passion but only they who exclude themselves."[12]

The statement that Arminianism is not Pelagianism needs a further word of emphasis. The theology Wesley inherited was a theology of grace. Certain modern writers, as well as some ancient ones, have believed that man can of his own natural abilities achieve his salvation. This is not of the main stream of Christian theology, and it was not a part of the High Church tradition of the Epworth household. Certain Arminians did become humanists; but, as Dr. Rupp pointed out in his Oxford paper of 1951, certain Calvinists became Unitarians, but there is no necessary connection between their former and their latter state. Bishop Beveridge in the seventeenth century had a fine phrase: "For my own part it is a greater happiness I expect when I am dead than I am able to deserve when I am alive."

When the Wesleys emphasized that salvation is by grace of God they were not testifying to some new theology, but repeating the doctrine of the church. There was no ambiguity in the Article: "We are accounted righteous before God, only for the merits

of our Lord and Saviour, Jesus Christ by Faith, and not
for our own works or deservings.... "

John Wesley, like the Calvinists, would argue from
the character of God when it came to this matter of God
foreordaining man to life and to death. But whereas the
Calvinists would argue from God's sovereign power,
Wesley would argue from His love. Therefore, in inter-
preting the favorite Scriptures in regard to the doctrine
of predestination Wesley does so interpret them. Eph.
1:5, "Having predestinated us to the adoption of sons,"
is explained as follows: "Having fore-ordained that all
who afterward believed should enjoy the dignity of
being sons of God and joint heirs with Christ." In commenting on Eph. 1:11, Wesley explains that God's will
is not arbitrary "but flowing from the rectitude of His
nature, else what security would there be that it would
be His will to keep His word even with the elect?"[13]

The abhorrence of the Wesleys for the doctrine of
predestination finds, naturally enough, its most violent
expression in some of Charles Wesley's hymns. One hesi-
tates to say "hymn" in this connection, but they are
included in his hymn books. In one hymn Charles comes
close to blasphemy:

> My dear Redeemer, and my God,
>   I stake my soul on Thy free grace;
> Take back my interest in Thy blood,
>   Unless it stream'd for *all* the race.

According to the Methodist belief this free grace of
Almighty God came to sinful man. That man is sinful
ought not to be news to a generation that has become
accustomed to novels and plays where half-wits and
prostitutes seem frequently to make up the larger part
of the cast. It ought not to be news to those who have
lived through two World Wars and have learned just

how tame the old phrase "man's inhumanity to man" really is. As a matter of fact the spiritual trauma which World War I inflicted upon so many people in the West, particularly in the United States, was produced by the belief in the first part of the twentieth century that no nation would again deliberately go out to make war upon another nation. The Ford peace ship which caused so much laughter on the part of the worldly-wise was a very sincere, if pathetic, gesture by those who simply did not believe that men in the twentieth century would deliberately kill each other.

Traditionally the church has not thought very highly of mankind. Article IX of the Church of England defined original sin as

The fault or corruption of the nature of every man, that naturally is engendered of the offspring of Adam, whereby man is very far gone from Original Righteousness, and is of his own nature inclined to evil, so that the Flesh lusteth always contrary to the Spirit . . .

This doctrine of original sin was taken very seriously. Arminius himself wrote in answer to one who had doubted that infants were capable of having rejected the grace of God and therefore deserved punishment for it:

You maintain the rejection of grace foreseen not to be the cause of desertion, because you say "infants dying without the Gospel covenant have not rejected grace" and yet are reprobate and deserted of God. But I say that they have rejected the grace of the Gospel in their parents, and grandparents, and forefathers, by which act they have deserved to be deserted by God.[14]

Some modern writers have assumed that our neglect of the doctrines of original sin is responsible for a good many of our troubles at the present time. There is no

doubt that a failure to realize the gravity of sin is a
major cause for any failure of religion in Christian terms.
But there have always been different explanations of
what is called original sin. One of the primary problems
is why do people sin at all, and one of the traditional
solutions has been that man in the person of Adam fell
away from original righteousness and thus entailed sin
upon all men.

There are times when Wesley talks about this in the
traditional terms. Man is far gone from original righteousness, and there is no good in him. Because Wesley
was a logician he found himself always involved in the
problem: How can a man sin unless there be sin in him?
As one of his best commentators explained a good while
ago, Wesley frequently thought of original sin as a
substance and looked forward to the time when that
substance might be removed. At the same time he was
never quite sure that people who had gotten rid of the
substance had achieved sinless perfection.

Someone has suggested that what is needed in the
explanation of Wesley is some explication of his doctrine of the fall and his reconciliation of this with Arminian theology. What Wesley did, whether it be reasonable or not, was to assert that the grace of God is
always with men unless it is completely rejected. Man in
a state of nature is totally depraved, but

there is no man that is in a state of mere nature; there is no
man, unless he has quenched the Spirit, that is wholly void
of the grace of God. No man living is entirely destitute of
what is vulgarly called natural conscience. But this is not
natural. It is more properly termed preventing grace ...
So that no man sins because he has not grace, but because he
does not use the grace which he hath.[15]

It might as well be said once and for all that Wesley,
the Oxford don who had specialized in logic, would not

have understood dialectical explanations of original sin. "The Christian doctrine of original sin," writes Professor Reinhold Niebuhr,

with its seemingly contradictory assertions about the inevitability of sin and man's responsibility for sin is a dialectical truth which does justice to the fact that man's self-love and self-centredness is inevitable, but not in such a way as to fit into the category of natural necessity. It is within and by his freedom that man sins.[16]

On the contrary, Wesley had to satisfy his eighteenth-century English mind, trained in Oxford logic, that man could fall in Adam and yet be responsible for his sins. And the explanation had to be in terms that a High Churchman could approve. This explanation he found in the doctrine of preventing grace.

The grace that prevents, or goes before, is simply Wesley's and the traditional term for the grace of God that comes to all men. William Cannon notes that there is a resemblance between Bishop Butler's idea of conscience and John Wesley's preventing grace. Wesley's insistence upon preventing grace is, of course, aimed at avoiding the necessity of accepting the Calvinistic doctrine of irresistible grace. If man is totally depraved so that there is no good in him, if this natural man is incapable of responding to the call of the gospel, then there is only one possibility for his salvation: that irresistible grace may take hold of him.

Since Wesley did not believe in irresistible grace and since he did not want to surrender his belief that any man has enough of the grace of God to respond to the call of the gospel, his explanation is sensible enough. He at least makes it very clear that he is not preaching that men may of their own efforts achieve salvation. He is insisting that men must find salvation through the

Grace of God, but he will not shut out from this grace any of the children of men.

As we have already seen, present salvation—peace, joy, and righteousness in the Holy Spirit—comes to the man who trusts God. And this man usually is aware of the fact that he is trusting God and has the assurance at least of present salvation. But Wesley believed that the important step that was taking place at that moment was not simply the pardoning of a man's sins but what he called the new birth. This was the beginning of a new life which was to work in man until his final salvation in the next world.

Wesley thought it was very important to distinguish justification, the work that God does *for* us, from sanctification, the work that God does *in* us. Actually he was emphasizing the two beliefs concerning the mode of salvation to which he held tenaciously: salvation by faith and "without holiness no man shall see the Lord." Wesley's passion for Christian perfection never allowed him to deviate from the belief that man must sometime or other be inwardly and outwardly holy.

One aspect of Wesley's doctrine of Christian perfection or perfect love was of course manifested and has been manifested through the years in the various "Holiness" sects which have sprung up from time to time inside Methodism and without. There is no question of the honesty of the people who are thus interested in what is a legitimate part of the Christian faith. Generally it took the form of what is called the second blessing. This has a genuine root in the preaching of the Wesleys. If a man is delivered from his sins by the pardoning love of God on the condition that he trusts in God through Jesus Christ, he should look forward to a deliverance from all sin, especially from original sin, by his trust in Christ. This is the second blessing.

Some of the Wesleys' finer hymns have to do with this particular experience.

There is of course in all such emphasis upon perfection the constant danger of spiritual pride. And there is a particular kind of irritating goodness which sometimes goes with this kind of claim which has made it especially difficult to deal with these groups. But one must realize that there have been some beautiful and humble characters which have adorned this doctrine of Christian perfection. One can only pay tribute to those who quietly and with no spiritual pride have believed that they have reached this stage of perfect love.

Apparently Wesley came more and more to believe that it is not well to speak of justified states or of sanctified states. He did not entirely free himself of the idea that the Christian life is a series of stages, or one might almost say terraces. One ascends from the lower to the higher. But Wesley realized the fact that these so-called states are not plateaus and that in some way the figures of speech used to describe them are not accurate.

Here is where Wesley's doctrine of moment by moment is also applicable. He believed that a man might receive his "second blessing" by faith. And his most valuable insight in this connection perhaps is that in any one moment a man may have perfect love.

The truth about the matter is that Wesley is in this instance falling back upon the age-long belief that the grace of God infused into mankind makes him a new creature. Wesley is clear when he is talking to men who are obviously not theologians. His two *Appeals to Men of Reason and Religion* are in many ways his best expression, although a good part of these tracts is taken up, as usual, with the endless meeting of arguments sentence by sentence. Wesley defines pure religion as love to God and man. He believes, according to several

statements in various places, that conversion is the
beginning of the sanctification of a man, and he thinks
that normally a man ought to go on progressing in
the Christian life until the day of death. Nevertheless, he always holds to the possibility of an instantaneous sanctification. Wesley himself never claimed
the experience. That he did know some who had had it,
he claims very definitely, although there is little evidence
except the accounts by the people themselves.

What Wesley did insist upon, however, was this constant holiness of life, a holiness both inward and
outward. And because of this he was being accused
very frequently of preaching salvation by works. It is
well known that in the 1770's he brought out at one of
the conferences and published in the Minutes statements which aroused a very severe doctrinal controversy
with those Methodists whose leanings were toward
Calvinism. It is not always known, however, that he was
accused of preaching salvation by works even at the
beginning.

Wesley says that when he and his brother began
to preach justification by faith they were astonished
to find that they were accused of preaching justification
by works. He did not understand why this accusation
was made until he found out later that under strict
interpretation of the doctrine of election man was supposed to have been saved without even faith as a
condition. If one insists upon faith as a condition one is
insisting upon works.

Wesley has a great many ways in which to argue
about this, too. The eighteenth century had ceased to
have bloody battles about religion, but it did not cease
to have battles of words. Wesley himself claimed always
to be either distressed or bored with argument: "Oh that
I might dispute with no man!"[17] But it is doubtful

whether Wesley would have been happy without the
opportunity to exercise his logic now and again. Works
are necessary for final salvation *as a condition.* They are
not necessary *as a meritorious requirement.* To the edi-
tor of the *London Magazine* Wesley wrote in 1760:

In the seventh [he is referring to the paragraphs of the
article against which he is writing] you grant "that works are
not meritorious unless accompanied with faith." No nor then
neither. But pray do not talk of this any more till you know
the difference between meritorious and rewardable; otherwise your ignorance will cause you to blunder along without
shame and without end.[18]

The truth about the matter is that Wesley himself
got to the point where he considered this quibbling
about words more or less unnecessary. In 1770 he quit
talking about the difference between a material and a
necessary condition, or the difference between meritorious and rewardable. The famous Minutes of 1770
need to be quoted at some length:

Q. 74 What is the direct antidote to Methodism, the doctrine of heart holiness?

A. Calvinism: All the devices of Satan, for these fifty
years have done far less toward stopping the work of God,
than that single doctrine. It strikes at the root of salvation
from sin, previous to Glory, putting the matter on quite
another issue.

Q. 75 But wherein lie the charms of this doctrine? What
makes men swallow it so greedily?

A. (1) It seems to magnify Christ; although in reality it
supposes Him to have died in vain. For the absolutely elect
must have been saved without Him; and the non-elect cannot be saved by Him.

(2) It is highly pleasing to flesh and blood, final persever-
ance in particular.

Q. 77 We said in 1744 "We have learned too much toward
Calvinism." Wherein?

A. (1) With regard to man's faithfulness ...

(2) With regard to "working for life," which our Lord expressly commands us to do. "Labour," literally *work*, "for the meat that endureth to everlasting life." And in fact every believer, till he comes to Glory, works *for* as well as *from* life.

(3) We have received it as a maxim, that "a man is to do nothing in order to justification." Nothing can be more false. Whoever desires to find favour with God, should "cease from evil, and learn to do well." So God himself teaches by the Prophet Isaiah. Whoever repents, should "do works meet for repentance." And if this is not in order to find favour, what does he do them for?

Once more review the whole affair:

(1) Who of us is now accepted of God?

He that now believes in Christ with a loving, obedient heart.

(2) But who among those that never heard of Christ?

He that according to the light he has, "fears God and worketh righteousness."

(3) Is this the same with "he that is sincere?"

Nearly, if not quite.

(4) Is not this salvation by works?

Not by the merit of works, but by works as a condition.

(5) What have we then been disputing about for these thirty years?

I am afraid about words, namely, in some of the foregoing instances.

(6) As to merit itself, of which we have been so dreadfully afraid: We are rewarded "according to our works," yea "because of our works." How does this differ from "for the sake of our works"? And how differs this from *secundum meritis operum?* Which is no more than "as our works deserve." Can you split this hair? I doubt I cannot.

For many years the accepted interpretation of Wesley's doctrine on this point was in Fletcher's *Checks to Antinomianism*. That used to be the staple of every Methodist preacher's library. In regard to these Minutes Fletcher said definitely:

For my part I entirely agree with the author of the Minutes, and thank him for daring to break the ice of prejudice and bigotry among us, by restoring *works of righteousness* to their deserved glory, without detracting from the glory of "the Lord our righteousness." I am as much persuaded that the grace of Christ *merits* in the works of his members ... though it is mixed with dust and dross, which are good for nothing. ... There is but one man whose works are truly meritorious; but when he works in us by his Spirit, our works cannot, (so far as he is concerned in them,) but be in a sense meritorious; because they are his works.[19]

Wesley said when he ordained preachers for America and recapitulated his views:

Undoubtedly faith is the work of God; and yet it is the duty of men to believe. And every man may believe if he will, though not when he will. If he seeks faith in the appointed ways, sooner or later the power of the Lord will be present, whereby (1) God works, and by His power (2) man believes. In order of thinking God's working goes first; but not in order of time. Believing is the act of the human mind, strengthened by the power of God.[20]

Wesley took certain positions which were somewhat horrifying to the people of his day, and as a matter of fact are not readily accepted by many people at the present time. In the first place, what happens to those people who do not believe in a cardinal doctrine such as justification by faith? In 1767 Wesley said it appeared clear as day that "a mystic, who denies Justification by Faith (Mr. Law for instance) may be saved." Of course, this brought him immediately face to face with the question, is the doctrine of Justification by Faith then the article by which the church stands or falls? And he decided that if a man could be saved without believing in Justification by Faith "is it not high time for us to 'reject bombast and words half a yard

long,' and to return to the plain word, 'he that feareth
God and worketh righteousness, is accepted of Him'? "[21]

In the Minutes quoted above the question had been
raised about those who never heard of Christ. This was
the old question about the salvation of the heathen.
The view accepted generally was that the good works
of the heathen were merely splendid sins, and therefore
there was not much worry about their condition.
But in the Minutes it was answered that those who
had never heard of Christ were accepted according to
the light that they had, if they feared God and worked
righteousness. But this brought up the question, is not
this the same as being sincere? The answer was, "Nearly,
if not quite."

At an earlier time in the Minutes of 1746 it had been
declared that an unbeliever who was sincere "if he per-
severe therein, God will infallibly give him faith."
A year later the question was discussed somewhat more
extensively:

Men may have many good tempers and a blameless life
(speaking in a loose sense), by nature and habit, with preventing grace; and yet not have faith and the love of God. It is
scarce possible for us to know all the circumstances relating
to such persons, as to judge certainly concerning them. But
this we know, if Christ is not revealed in them they are not
yet Christian believers.

Later the question is asked, "But what will become of
them then, suppose they die in this state?" The answer
is simply that we do not suppose anything of the kind.
Men either go backward or forward. "If they continue
to seek, they will surely find righteousness and peace
with joy in the Holy Ghost. We are confirmed in this
belief by the many instances we have seen of such as
these finding peace at the last hour." As we have seen,

Wesley finally came to feel there was a hope not only that a sincere man would be eventually brought to the light, but that he would be saved in the Last Day without necessarily having clear conceptions about salvation or even believing in Justification by Faith.

It has frequently been the fashion among writers to talk about American Methodism as given over entirely to the social gospel. There is much truth in this, and we have perhaps been guilty of careless thinking and undue emphasis upon works, as if they alone could merit our salvation. In recent years when the Continental confessional theologies have found favor in this country, either in their original forms or as translated by our own theologians, it has become particularly the fashion to decry the activities of the church as stressing works instead of the Protestant Reformation doctrines which presumably Wesley restored to power.

But it might as well be understood that actually the Methodists have grounds for their belief in the importance of good works. Our notion of good works and eighteenth-century notions may not coincide, but there is no question whatsover that during all his life Wesley insisted that man could resist the Spirit of God if he chose to do so. Moreover, he believed that man would finally be judged—and I mean *finally,* because Wesley distinguished between final and present salvation—by his works. He believed, of course, in the constant necessity of faith; but for ordinary purposes, not for justification, he defined faith as man's insight into the eternal world. He drew long parallels between the child being born into a new world and the spiritual man who walked in this world after his new birth.

It must be admitted, however, that the Methodists in their activity have gone far afield from those things in which the early Methodists were interested. The early

Methodists were interested in the souls of men, and
their concern for man's material condition arose out of a
belief that it is our duty to help one another and that in
that helping we should have in mind not only the immediate relief of want but preparation for the future. This
latter was especially instanced in the lending of money to
workmen with which to buy their tools. But there was
no interest in influencing government to relieve men's
condition. Especially was there no interest in such
activity as designed to influence men's souls.

In this we can say that the early Methodists were
shortsighted, or that they simply partook of the views of
their century. But it would be a fatal misinterpretation
of the Methodist missionary message if we did not
remember that always it was a religious message.
And Wesley's notion, which persisted for many years
in this country as well as in England, was that men
should attempt to use the grace of God as it came to
them through the means. The phrase "means of grace"
is an old ecclesiastical phrase. It came into the English
Prayer Book in 1662 in the General Thanksgiving, "For
the means of grace and the hope of Glory." It was a
common usage so far as Wesley is concerned, and he has
one of the sermons that are listed as standard on
"The Means of Grace." He defines the means of grace as
follows: "outward signs, words, or actions, ordained of
God, and appointed for this end, to be the ordinary
channels whereby He might convey to men, preventing,
justifying, or sanctifying grace."[22]

It is evident that here is the danger of conceiving
grace in a material sense which is to be obtained through
means. But when Wesley comes to explain what he
means by the phrase, this objection is removed.

The chief of these means are prayer, whether in secret or
with the great congregation; searching the scriptures (which

implies reading, hearing and meditating thereon); and receiving the Lord's Supper, eating bread and drinking wine in remembrance of Him; and these we believe to be ordained of God, as the ordinary channels of conveying His grace to the souls of men.

Sugden, in commenting on this,[23] remarks that baptism is omitted because most of those to whom Wesley was preaching this sermon had already been baptized in infancy. This is a probable explanation, since it is apparent that Wesley's views concerning the grace of God in baptism were rather definite—although before his death he seems to have moved away from his earlier position of baptismal regeneration.

When he says "means of grace," he means exactly what he says. He rebukes some of his followers for not studying the Bible. He has no sympathy, as he showed in his sermon on "Enthusiasm," with the notion that people may know what is in the Bible simply by the inspiration of the Spirit. And Sugden brought together in his comments on the sermon on "The Means of Grace" some remarks on Wesley's views on the Bible which are apropos at the present time.[24] Wesley talks at times as if he believed that every word of Scripture is infallible. "If there be any mistakes in the Bible, there may as well be a thousand. If there be one falsehood in that Book, it did not come from the God of truth."[25] But he insists that the Bible which was in the hands of most of his people, what we call the Authorized Version, is not itself infallible, remarking at one time[26] that "many such emendations there are in this translation; one would think King James had made them himself!"[27] When Wesley came to provide the service for the American Methodists, he left out certain Psalms which he considered unfit for Christian lips.

As to the other means of grace, particularly the Lord's

Supper, something has already been said about Wesley's own practice. It has been sometimes forgotten that the early Methodists believed that the Sacrament of the Lord's Supper was a converting ordinance. Susannah Wesley was said to have been converted during her reception of the Lord's Supper. And there has been much discussion about this particular part of Wesley's belief. Nevertheless, there seems to be good evidence for the use of the Lord's Supper in early Methodism as a converting ordinance. To *Hymns on the Lord's Supper* by John and Charles Wesley, which was printed in 1745, there was prefaced an extract from Dr. Brevint:

Hitherto we have considered this Holy Sacrament both as a *memorial* of the death of Christ, and as sign of those graces wherewith He sustains and nourishes believing souls. But this is not all: for both the end of the Holy Communion, the wants and desires of those who receive it, and the strength of other places of Scripture, require, that much more be contained therein than a bare *memorial* or *representation*. (1) The end of the Holy Communion, which is to make us partakers of Christ in another manner than when we only hear His word; (2) the wants and desires of those who receive it, who seek not a bare *representation* or remembered representation. I want and seek my Saviour Himself and I haste to this Sacrament for the same purpose that Saint Peter and John hasted to His sepulchre; because I hope to find Him there.

In another place Brevint has put succinctly his view of the importance of the Lord's Supper:

Of these blessings Christ from above is pleased to bestow sometimes more, sometimes less, in the several ordinances of His church, which as the stars in Heaven differ from each other in glory. Fasting, prayer, hearing His word, are all good vessels to draw water from this well of salvation; but they are not all equal. The Holy Communion, when well

used, exceeds as much in blessings as it exceeds in danger
of a curse when wickedly and irreverently taken.

The Wesleys put this last paragraph into verse.

> Fasting He doth, and hearing bless,
>   And prayer can much avail,
> Good vessels all to draw the grace
>   Out of salvation's well.
>
> But none, like this mysterious rite
>   Which dying mercy gave,
> Can draw forth all His promised might
>   And all His will to save.

In more than one hymn it is made clear that the Sacrament is for sinners as well as for saints.

> Now in the means that grace impart,
>   Whisper peace into my heart;
> Appear the Justifier
>   Of all who to Thy wounds would fly,
> And let me have my own desire
>   And see Thy face and die.

One of the longest of the hymns for the Lord's Supper
speaks in no uncertain terms about the belief of the
early Methodists in regard to the way in which they
should expect the grace of God.

> Not then above their Master wise
>   They simply in His paths remain'd,
> And called to mind His sacrifice
>   With steadfast faith and love unfeign'd
> With Jesu's constant presence blest,
>   While duteous to His dying word,
> They kept the Eucharistic feast
>   And supp'd in Eden with their Lord.
> Why is the faithful seed decreased,
>   The life of God extinct and dead?
> The daily sacrifice is ceased,
>   And charity to Heaven is fled.

If this suggests to anyone that Wesley was going back to a materialistic conception of the grace of God it is well to ponder one of the last paragraphs in his sermon on "The Means of Grace":

Remember also, to use all means *as means;* as ordained, not for their own sake, but in order to the renewal of your soul in righteousness and true holiness. If, therefore, they actually tend to this, well; but if not, they are dung and dross.

And there is another paragraph in this same sermon making his position very clear:

Settle this in your heart, that the *opus operatum,* the mere *work done,* profiteth nothing; that there is no *power* to save but in the Spirit of God, no *merit* but in the blood of Christ; that, consequently, even what God ordains, conveys no grace to the soul, if you trust not in Him alone. On the other hand, he that does truly trust in Him cannot fall short of the grace of God, even though he were cut off from every outward ordinance, though he were shut up in the center of the earth.

CHAPTER FIVE

ON THE CHURCH AND MINISTRY

JOHN WESLEY's teaching concerning church and ministry has been neglected. There are doubtless many reasons for this, but I think one is that at certain times the Methodists have not wanted to publicize their founders' views, since the modern Methodists have not always shared those views. Another reason is that discussions over Wesley's opinions on the church and ministry have usually arisen when the Methodists have been under attacks from other churches. It is true that Bishop John Amory's well-known "A Defense of 'Our Fathers' " was called forth by internal discussions in the Methodist church; but the arguments were aimed at those members of the Protestant Episcopal church who doubted the validity of Methodist organizations. In England, toward the middle of the last century, as a result of the Oxford Movement certain High-Churchmen rediscovered John Wesley and claimed him for their own. To rebut their claims, Methodists in England were inclined to emphasize only the extreme Protestant positions of their founder.

What did Wesley himself think about the church and

the ministry? There is no question about his early views.
In 1745 he wrote a letter to his brother-in-law, West-
ley Hall, who had written urging John and Charles to
renounce the Church of England. In this letter (written
in December, 1745) Wesley makes clear his views:

We believe it would not be right for us to administer either
Baptism or the Lord's Supper unless we had a commission
so to do from those bishops whom we apprehend to be in a
succession from the apostles. And yet we allow these bishops
are the successors of those who were dependent on the
Bishop of Rome.

We believe there is, and always was, in every Christian
Church (whether dependent on the Bishop of Rome or
not), an outward priesthood, ordained by Jesus Christ, and
an outward sacrifice offered therein, by men authorized to
act as ambassadors of Christ and stewards of the myster-
ies of God. . . .

We believe that the three-fold order of ministers . . . is not
only authorized by the apostolical institution, but also by
the written word.[1]

It is frequently assumed that John Wesley's conversion in May, 1738, changed him from a High-Churchman to an evangelical or Low-Churchman with evangelical views. Apparently this cannot be true if we are
to assume that part of John Wesley's High-Churchman-
ship was contained in his views of the church and the
ministry. Eight and a half years after the conversion
John Wesley was asserting that he believed in apostolical succession and that men must be episcopally
ordained if they were rightfully to administer the
sacraments.

A little while after this (on January 20, 1746, to be
exact) Wesley read Lord Peter King's *Account of the
Primitive Church.* He had previously, in the letter to
Hall, declared himself ready to hear argument; and

apparently he was impressed by Lord King's account. He says, indeed:

In spite of the vehement prejudice of my education, I was ready to believe that this was a fair and impartial draught; but, if so, it would follow that bishops and presbyters are (essentially) of one order, and that originally every Christian congregation was a church independent of all others.[2]

This is one of the instances frequently cited to show that Wesley was in the habit of reading a book and without much thought adopting its conclusions. The other example is the better-known instance of Wesley reading Dr. Johnson's pamphlet, *Taxation, No Tyranny*. I flatter myself that in the book I wrote several years ago, *The Lord's Horseman*, I explained the Johnson pamphlet in a reasonable fashion.[3]

The truth is that neither instance proves the contention that Wesley was a thoughtless reader given to reflecting what he had last read. In this case, Wesley had for many years been reviewing his High Church assumptions. On his return from America he had gone over his experience and decided that he had himself leaned too heavily on the early church and its example. He had decided that some of the documents on which he had relied were not as early as he had thought they were. It might be said that in this—for example in the matter of the date of the *Apostolic Constitutions*—Wesley was in line with modern scholarship. In the second place, Wesley had been associating with men who were not episcopally ordained, and learning something of practical Christian character. He was, in other words, prepared to be impressed by Lord Peter King's emphasis on the oneness of the presbyters and bishops in the early church.

It is generally conceded that the Bible itself does

not make it clear that there was an original distinction between presbyters and bishops. Lord King laid considerable emphasis upon the testimony of Jerome (340?-420) concerning the Church of Alexandria. The passage in Jerome follows:

> For even at Alexandria, from the time of Mark the Evangelist to the episcopates of Heraclas and Dionysius, the presbyters used always to appoint as bishop one chosen out of their number, and placed on the higher grade, as if an army should make a commander, or as if deacons should choose one of themselves whom they should know to be diligent, and call him archdeacon. For, with the exception of ordaining, what does a bishop do which a presbyter does not?[4]

Jerome's well-known anti-Roman feelings must be taken into account, and of late years the testimony concerning Alexandria has been frequently discounted. But to Wesley, as to Lord King, this was only additional evidence confirming the New Testament.

The conclusions to which Wesley came—whether they are correct or not is for scholars to continue to argue about—were these:

In the first place, he never failed in his estimation of the Church of England as the best-organized national church in the world. He accepted her doctrines (as he understood them) and her worship.

He never doubted the right of lay preachers to preach as extraordinary messengers with divine calls.

He never doubted that ministers or pastors should have orders from the church as well as an inner call. These must be sent as well as called.

He did decide that episcopal ordination, in the sense that the Church of England understood it, was not necessary.

Wesley's views on orders may be seen in his *Notes on*

the New Testament. Commenting on the opening verses of I Tim. 4, Wesley said: "But where are the presbyters? Were this order essentially distinct from that of bishop, should the apostle have passed it over in silence?" In commenting on Acts 20:17, Wesley said that the elders of a church "are called bishops in the twenty-eighth verse [rendered *overseers* in our translation]. Perhaps elders and bishops were then the same; or no otherwise different than are the rector of the parish and his curate."

Wesley's *Notes on the New Testament* was published in 1755. That he did not change his mind in his essential views of the Christian ministry is evidenced by a sermon he preached in 1789 at Cork, Ireland. It has become well known as the Korah sermon, as it is based upon the fourth verse of the fifth chapter of Hebrews: "No man taketh this honor unto himself, but he that is called of God, as was Aaron." In this sermon Wesley discusses the office of preacher and the office of priest, and maintains that they have always been distinct both in the Old Testament and in the New. His views, as will be seen, are set forth in much the same terms that he has used for thirty or forty years. It is suggested by many that his sermons, as his ordinations, were the works of an old and failing mind. It would be a little difficult for Methodists in America to accept this explanation; for if Wesley was senile in 1789, there could be some reason to think that his powers might have been failing in 1784. But his statements of the ministerial office in 1789 are very similar to those that he made nearly a third of a century before, and in the very height of the progress of Methodism. In the Korah sermon Wesley says:

In ancient times the office of a Priest and that of a Preacher were known to be entirely distinct. . . .

Many learned men have shown at large that our Lord

himself, and all his Apostles, built the Christian Church as
nearly as possible on the plan of the Jewish. So the Great
High Priest of our profession sent Apostles and Evangelists
to proclaim glad tidings to all the world; and then Pastors,
Preachers and Teachers, to build up in the faith the congregations that should be founded. But I do not find that
ever the office of an Evangelist was the same as that of a
Pastor, frequently called a Bishop. He presided over the
flock, and administered the sacraments: the former assisted
him, and preached the word, either in one or more congregations. I cannot prove from any part of the New Testament, or from any author of the three first centuries, that the
office of an Evangelist gave any man a right to act as a
Pastor or a Bishop. I believe these offices were considered
as quite distinct from each other till the time of Constantine.

Wesley goes on to explain that when he used lay
preachers he used them as extraordinary messengers
"raised up to provoke the ordinary ones to jealousy."
So he sent them out to preach and to preach in such
places as he ordered. At no time, he claimed, did he
ever send them out to administer the sacraments.
He sums up his position as follows:

I wish all of you who are vulgarly termed Methodists would
seriously consider what has been said. And particularly you
whom God hath commissioned to call sinners to repentance.
It does by no means follow from hence, that you are commissioned to baptize, or to administer the Lord's Supper.
Ye never dreamed of this, for ten or twenty years after ye
began to preach. Ye did not then like Korah, Dathan, Abilal,
"seek the priesthood also." Ye knew, "no man taketh this
honor unto himself, but he that is called of God, as was
Aaron."

The Korah sermon seems to make it very evident that
while Wesley had discarded his belief in the three
orders, he had never discarded his belief in two orders
of the ministry; and especially had he not discarded

his belief in a difference between the extraordinary messengers sent only to preach and to evangelize and those who were sent to act as pastors or bishops of one or more churches.

It is apparent that Wesley, believing as he did that presbyters and bishops were of the same order and had the same right to ordain, performed his ordinations for America in that belief. It is, of course, not possible to believe that these orders were presbyterian, since that would have required not simply the ordination by presbyters, but presbyters acting with authority. Wesley and his helpers did not have authority from any organized body of the church such as is necessary for a presbyterian ordination. Of course, he did not have authority from the Church of England to act in the capacity of a bishop. Orders he believed to be essentially those of a presbyter. But where does he get his authority? Dr. Edgar W. Thompson has suggested in a recent book, *John Wesley: Apostolic Man,* that Wesley was acting as did the early apostles under direct divine guidance. This is probably what Wesley himself believed, and it is difficult to contest the facts. Wesley had, he believed under providence, control over a large body of believers both in the United Kingdom and in America. No one else exercised this control, the preservation of doctrine, that is the teaching faculty, discipline, direction of religious life: in short, the practical functions of a bishop less ordination. Since Wesley believed that ordination did not pose a problem of order, it was normal that finally he should take it upon himself to act in his capacity of what he called a "scriptural bishop." It is not to be denied that Wesley's ordinations for the United Kingdom pose a different problem. It is difficult to see why these were emergencies he had to meet in the same sense in which there was an emergency in America.

As to whether the American Methodists followed out Wesley's intention, there have been arguments and arguments. The truth seems to be that the church in America followed out Wesley's intention, but not his words. He did not want to use the word *bishop* any more than he wanted to use the word *presbyter*. But he made all provision for an American church on the model of the Church of England. There seems little doubt that he made the preparations for the setting up of this church, as he made the preparations for the setting up of an independent British Methodism, intending to preserve the forms of a church plus the spiritual life of the Methodist movement. If the Methodists in America offended him by their use of the word *bishop* and by their touchiness about Wesley's domination, the fact remains that the Methodist church in America does carry out what seemed to have been the intentions that Wesley manifested.

All this throws considerable light, it would seem, upon the discussions between the Anglican churches and the nonepiscopal churches concerning either union or full intercommunion. There is no doubt that the Methodist church in America, and of this alone we can speak here, does believe in both the inward and the outward call for the work of the ministry. The inward call the Methodist church understands, but the outward call is symbolized by ordination at the hands of a Methodist bishop.

There is little point in arguing about diocesan episcopacy, because so far as the jurisdiction of the bishop is concerned the Methodists in America have had diocesan episcopacy for many, many years. There has been no general superintendency in the original sense of the word since frontier days. It is obviously impossible for any bishop now to cover the entire church, and the simple provision that he could be called from one end of the church to the other is, to say the least, a formal recognition of the principle of an itinerant episcopacy rather than any practical application of it.

The dioceses over which the bishops in the Methodist church preside are, of course, larger than those of the Protestant Episcopal church—or, so far as I know, of any other Anglican body. In truth, these areas are too large for any efficient administration; and either the Methodist church will have to face the handing over of all administrative matters to boards and committees and organizational agencies of one kind or another, or it will have to increase the number of bishops until they are able to administer effectively the areas they have. One instance of this is in our cities. We shift our bishops every four or eight years usually, and as a consequence a Methodist bishop does not stay in an American city long enough to be recognized by the city itself. As a result Protestantism is frequently represented by the Protestant Episcopal bishop, who probably does not have a tithe of the members that the Methodist bishop has. The increase of the number of Methodist bishops is a burning practical problem.

We, of course, will have to satisfy ourselves as to what we mean by apostolical succession, if we are to come to any meeting of minds with the Protestant Episcopal or other Anglican bodies. As the Canadian Anglican, R. F. Hettlinger, has asserted recently,

To those of us who recognize in the Reformation a decisive reaffirmation of the Gospel, the Protestant communions represent a recovery of the apostolical succession through the vital life of the Church in circumstances in which the Episcopal succession had denied it. As Bishop Simon Patrick of Ely wrote in 1687 in defense of the theology of the Anglican Reformation: "Who dare say that this is a new religion, which is as old as Christ and the Apostles? With whom

whosoever agree, they are truly ancient Churches, though of
no longer standing than yesterday; as they that disagree with
those are new, though they can run up their pedigree to the
very Apostles."[5]

This is asserting essentially the Methodist position:
that apostolical succession consists in the succession of
doctrine and of worship. This we do believe, and we
maintain apostolical succession as a vital truth and one
to which we subscribe; but we cannot subscribe to an
apostolical succession which is purely an organizational
matter and rests upon evidence which, as Wesley said,
was never proved and can never be proved. Hettlinger
quotes Canon Quick as saying: "All our orders are in
part defective because none of them has the authoriza-
tion of the whole Church."[6] Hettlinger thinks that Dom
Gregory Dix implies the same thing on the ground that
in the early church free elections and acceptances by
the laity were as much a *sine qua non* of episcopal
authority as consecration, and that these parts of episcopal authority have been omitted largely since the Middle Ages. On the ground that all orders are in some way
or other defective, the Methodist church can stand with
her Anglican brethren. If reordination is a mutual
matter, entered into in good faith in order to extend the
area in which Christians of like views can minister, as
has been done in the South India church and is pro-
posed particularly in the Ceylon plans and the plan for
North India, then there could seem to be no objection,
other than prejudices, against our entering into schemes
of this kind for full intercommunion with the Anglican
bodies. One thing is certain: on the strength of our history we belong with the churchly churches. The Episcopal churches which represent the kind of government
the churches have had for some fifteen hundred years,
and probably had to a large extent in the early church,

are the ones with which the Methodist church has greatest affiliation.

The burden of arguments for centuries has been as to the presence or absence in the early church of episcopacy. The lines have been pretty fairly drawn, and there is not much chance that anything new can be said. Only one new thing has been added in recent years. The discovery of the Dead Sea Scrolls does show that there were in existence at the time of our Lord certain administrative arrangements among the communities in the Dead Sea region that would have given precedent for episcopal government in the early church. In other words, the assumption has been made for many years that episcopacy was too highly developed as a form of government to have been begun in the early church. Certain passages in the *Manual of Discipline* and others of the Dead Sea Scrolls indicate that there was a ruling elder whose authority and jurisdiction was supplemented by twelve laymen corresponding to a large degree with what seems to be reflected in certain of the pastoral epistles of the New Testament: what Wesley calls the relation between a curate and his vicar.

Whether or not it can be shown that the episcopacy was an original element of church government, it certainly was very early; and most of the essential elements, with the exception of the reservation of ordination to the bishop, appear in Methodist episcopacy.

If we stand in the true apostolical succession of doctrine and worship, and if by mutual arrangement and understanding we can broaden the circle of those who come within the fellowship of full communion, proposals to that purpose are certainly to be taken in good faith.

Nevertheless, we as Methodists cannot be true to our

heritage if we enter into any scheme either for inter-communion or for union which requires us to renounce the validity of our own ministry. I realize that at the present time words like validity are being avoided, but the fact remains that if the only real and full ministry must come from the hands of those who stand in apostolical succession, conceived as a direct historical and factual line from the apostles, we Methodists must refuse to pay any such price no matter how attractive the extension of our influence and fellowship.

CHAPTER SIX

THE GENIUS OF METHODISM

THE CLASSIFYING of religious groups and movements is one of the occupational diseases of theologians and historians. It is an entirely legitimate effort, although it offers a full share of the difficulties which beset every endeavor to classify human beings. There are some particular hurdles.

In the first place, it is hard for a theologically oriented writer to see just what touches off certain practical movements. On the other side, practical-minded men have difficulty in grasping the convolutions of theological thought when it tries to grapple with problems of sin and redemption, of the nature of man and of God. I would not want to generalize about nationalities, but it is fair to remind ourselves that the English-speaking people have not been prolific in metaphysicians. On the other hand, Germany has produced metaphysicians and pure scientists. Their value is not to be disputed, but their best interpreters have not usually been Englishmen or Americans.

In the next place, when dealing with the Wesleyan movement it is not usually realized that John Wesley's work is complicated by several factors. In the first place, he was insatiably curious about human experience. He would read innumerable letters and journals and listen ad infinitum to stories of religious experience that would turn the average modern into a candidate for the nearest asylum. Moreover, Wesley would seldom rule out as impossible anything that was claimed by some as their experience unless he thought the experiences were clearly contrary to the Bible or to his own logical conception of reason. The result is that historians and other commentators on Methodism frequently turn up with some strange doctrines which they are convinced are authentically Methodist. This is particularly true since most church historians—including many Methodists—regard the Methodist Revival as an incident, more or less minor, in the history of modern Christendom.

Another difficulty in trying to place Methodism neatly on some theological shelf is that many neglect the simple fact that John Wesley lived a long time. He died sixty-five years after he was elected a fellow of Lincoln. In that time he read constantly, traveled extensively for an eighteenth-century Englishman, and consorted with all sorts and conditions of men. As a result he kept his mind hospitable to some strange theological guests, but he did try in his later years to order his thoughts and review his experiences.

Another of the hurdles in the path of any interpreter of Wesley is that the movement which is called Methodist took and has taken many forms which have no counterpart in the life of its founder. There have been Holiness movements, balancing always on the verge of Antinomianism, which could justify themselves by some words of John Wesley and especially by the songs of Charles. The revivalistic movements which have for-

gotten the careful cure of souls that characterized the
original Wesleyan evangelistic effort are another instance of taking the part for the whole. Certainly the
Methodist church in America and, I strongly suspect,
the Methodist churches elsewhere would fall far short
of Wesley's ideas and ideals. They are either too secular
or too much like the Dissenters whom he frequently
liked personally but disliked as groups.

Reinhold Niebuhr classes Methodism as "pietistic
evangelistic."[1] This is in line with the views of many
of the older historians. McGiffert saw Methodism as a
part of the whole Pietistic movement.

Not too many people today know what Pietism was.
It was a movement in late seventeenth- and early eighteenth-century Germany which revived the Lutheran
church and put its emphasis upon personal piety, upon
inward holiness, and upon good works. As a matter of
fact, some of the influence of Pietism on Methodism was
in this matter of works. The hospitals, orphanages, and
schools of the Pietists were models for those days.
Wesley, on his trip to Germany shortly after his conversion experience, was tremendously impressed with
what had been done. He had, of course, heard about
these things previously from the Moravians in Georgia.

Undoubtedly, too, Wesley learned from the Moravians to lay emphasis upon inward peace and inward
power over sin. There is no question that Wesley was
influenced not so much by Lutheranism as by the
Pietistic interpretation of Lutheranism.[2] The fact that
Methodism preached conversion can be traced, if one is
interested, both to the Puritans and to the Pietists.

There were specific incidents which led to the breaking off of Wesley's relations with the Moravians; but
there were inherent differences between them. Even in
the early days when he was debating with Count

Zinzendorf, Wesley was insisting upon holding the door open to the possibility of Christian Perfection. Zinzendorf was speaking of justification in much the terms which Wesley reserved for Perfection.

The Moravians thought that Wesley did not like them because they differed among themselves and because he could not rule. The Methodists also differed among themselves, but it is true enough that the official beliefs to be expressed by the leaders were determined by the Wesleys in "conference" with their brethren.

Essentially, however, the Moravians were too emotional. Some of their hymns revolted Wesley. They did not lay enough stress upon the lifelong search for holiness. The doctrine of good works as simply the natural and inevitable result of man's thankfulness for forgiveness was not enough. Wesley had much the attitude of Bishop Butler, who thought that natural good feeling might be sufficient for other people, but that Englishmen needed something more rigorous. Moreover, there were important elements of the Christian life which the Moravians did not emphasize as Wesley thought they should.

It may be that Methodism can be classified for some purposes as Pietistic; but if the Methodist movement in its essence be taken for what it was in the years when it made its first push in Britain and in America, the classification simply does not cover the facts.

Methodism has been taken by writers as an extension of Puritanism. This, of course, explains nothing, because the ideas of what Puritanism was and is are myriad. Dr. Rupp is right in saying that Macaulay's idea of a Puritan is nothing but a Victorian Evangelical in fancy dress.[3] A Puritan is now, as was frequently the case in the seventeenth century, taken to mean a precisian, a man who is considered as representative of what was known in this country as the bluenose Christian.

Of course, none of these caricatures is correct. The Puritans themselves were many of them members of the Church of England who objected to its rites and ceremonies as being too largely Romish. It is true that all those who rebelled against the Church of England in the seventeenth century have been lumped together as Puritans. In later years Dissent was understood as a descendant of Puritanism. Late scholars have been inclined to pick out certain characteristics of Puritanism in its pure sense as influencing Methodist life and practice. The belief that man lives in his vocation here, and that the true Christian works out his salvation in the common run of life rather than in monastic seclusion, is characteristic of Puritan attitudes and of Methodist attitudes. A belief in maintaining an economy of time and substance, shrinking from extravagance and ostentation, is characteristic of both groups. It has been pointed out, however, that the Methodist attitude toward economy of time and substance is also characteristic of a strain of piety coming down from High Church sources as well as from Puritanism.

What Methodists and non-Methodists are likely to forget is the Calvinistic Evangelical movement. In a recent series of lectures Professor John T. McNeill, a distinguished church historian, says it is remarkable that some historians refer to Wesley's conversion, in 1738, as the beginning of the Evangelical movement. Professor McNeill thinks that the Evangelical movement began earlier. As a matter of fact, this is a trend in recent writing. A book on the Evangelicals at Oxford traces their history to a time either prior to or simultaneous with Wesley's Holy Club, but emphasizes that the movement arose independently.

The fact is that we in the Methodist tradition have

neglected the Evangelical movement, which was characterized on the doctrinal side by Calvinism and on the side of church allegiance by both Church of England membership and dissenting connections.

Professor McNeill makes it very clear that the Evangelical movement with which he deals was Calvinistic. He quotes from an anonymous tract published in London in 1707 as throwing light on the doctrinal character of early Evangelicalism. The writer of this tract was sure that the sad condition of the Church of England was the result of the prevalence of Arminianism. The High-Churchmen "Debase the glory of God's grace and exalt pride in man."[4]

McNeill has written in a most illuminating fashion on the history of Evangelicalism. He thinks that the new element in Evangelicalism—and he notes that this was not new in the absolute sense—consisted "in the apostolic passion for the regeneration of individual souls and the spread of sincere Christian discipleship."[5] The Evangelicals, unlike the Puritans, were not interested primarily in a reform of churches. But McNeill thinks that most of what is significant in the Protestantism of the past two hundred years has "either been originated in or been revived by the Evangelical Revival."[6]

It would be well, therefore, to keep in mind that there was an evangelical movement distinct from that of the Wesleys. It is true that the Wesleys were better advertised, since the whole movement was dubbed by its opponents "Methodistic." Nevertheless, this Evangelical revival, which was in part separate from the Wesleyan movement, remained in the Church of England to form the Evangelical party which was so influential during the nineteenth century.

Wesley had great admiration for the Puritans, but he was thinking of Puritans as those divines who suf-

fered under Elizabeth I or those whose works he recom-
mended to his people. He did not once think of including in these recommendations the writings of Ranters
and Levellers or even Quakers. In his *Christian Library,*
the five-foot shelf of books which he edited for his
followers, Wesley included, along with Thomas à
Kempis, Jeremy Taylor, and Law, devotional works by
Bishop Hall, Richard Baxter, and Bunyan. It must be
confessed that he reprinted Bunyan's *Holy War* in an
abridged form. Wesley had excised what he considered
objectionable passages.

Wesley himself felt that the persecution of the Puritans in the time of Queen Elizabeth I was as bad as the
persecutions of Queen Mary in an earlier period. But he
was also amazed, as he said, at what he considered the
weakness of the Puritans, "many of whom spent so much
of their time and strength in disputing about surplices
and hoods, or kneeling at the Lord's Supper."[7]

When John Wesley included the works of Puritans
in his *Christian Library,* he declared that he admired
them for their spirit, for the fact that they exalted Christ,
the place that they gave to God's word, and the fact
that they tore up the roots of Antinomianism. He objected to the fact that they were controversial and ver-
bose, and sometimes "edited" them. He objected to the
fact, too, that they did not have a proper view of
sanctification.[8] It must be kept in mind that John Wesley
was not a Puritan in the classical sense of the term.
In Sermon LXI Wesley refers to those who complain
that the Reformation did not go far enough: it did not
"sufficiently reform the rites and ceremonies of the
Church." On this he comments: "Ye fools and blind!
To fix your whole attention on the circumstantials of
religion! Your complaint ought to have been, the essentials of religion were not carried far enough. You ought

vehemently to have insisted on an entire change of men's tempers and lives . . ."[9]

What, then, is the type of piety which characterized the Methodist missionary movement in its earliest days? I do not consider this the same as asking what type of piety characterizes Methodists today. It is not even the same as to ask what type of piety characterized the Methodist people in an earlier period. But the Methodist movement moved with unusual speed throughout the British Isles and throughout the southern colonies in America. What was being preached and what was the type of piety that was promoted?

It is easy to reply that it was an intensely emotional and highly individualistic religion. Enough has been said about the way in which Wesley's Societies and their discipline were connected with the evangelistic appeal to make it clear that this is a confusion of George White-field and later Methodist revivalists with John Wesley.

It is easy to see the whole movement as simply an evangelistic effort supplemented by devices to maintain a fever pitch of emotion. Or, in addition or instead, a movement to right the social wrongs of the new world just coming to a good beginning in the eighteenth century, by religious means.

All these views run up against hard facts. We have seen the essentially religious—not social—nature of Wesley's interests. And, whatever later Methodists might do, I cannot express Wesley's intentions better than I did some years ago: "As much as he was devoted to his Societies as voluntary associations for the promotion of holiness, he never for one moment thought of substituting a loose, edifying, disciplinary institution for the Church with its ministry and its sacraments."[10]

The truth is that all the easy cataloguing of the Wesleyan movement does not do justice to the variety and richness of it. Perhaps some would prefer to say that you have to deal with too many elements: an Oxford don who changed his mind about religious matters, including his own experience; people who could comprehend only the simplest statements; fanatics who had ecstatic experiences; ambitious preachers; a myriad of honest, striving people in faraway places both in Britain and in America.

Taking it by and large, there is only one way to deal with the question: What was the nature of Methodist religion? That is to describe it. It was not a syncretistic religion. It was rooted deep in Anglican piety and Anglican doctrine. But it belonged decidedly to one wing of that Anglican religion, which was so notoriously a compromise. It was not a Catholic counterattack, as Father Piette thought. The Catholic elements are there, but they are such Catholic elements as were indigenous to English religion. The Anglo-Catholic Revival of the nineteenth century was taken by friend and foe alike as too original. At least it was taken as having too few roots in the two centuries before it.

How, then, shall we describe the nature of the Wesleyan piety? In the first place there is no question that Wesley preached the necessity of conversion. There is no need to go into the doctrinal matters of what relation faith and repentance and the rest have to this matter of conversion. But Wesley was keenly aware of the sins of his time. Basil Willey points out that Wesley, along with others of entirely different beliefs, would not accept the optimism of the eighteenth century because he was too aware of the evils of society about him.[11]

Yet Wesley's teaching about man's sin was not a hopeless denunciation of men. There are indeed passages in his writings which would indicate that man is totally depraved and that there is no hope for him except by cataclysmic and irresistible action of the grace of God. But Wesley was a man who wrote much and talked much, and his writings must be compared with each other. Actually Willey is correct when he says that Wesley, along with Voltaire and Rousseau and others, rejected the optimism of the eighteenth century because it was a hopeless optimism.

It is ordinarily taken for granted that the optimism of the eighteenth century was a feeling that this world is the best of all possible worlds and that it will go on to perfection automatically. Actually, as Willey shows, eighteenth-century optimism was based on hopelessness. As Johnson put it: "All our effort ends in belief, that for the evils of life there is some good reason, and in confession, that the reason cannot be found."[12]

This is to say that the world about us is the best world that could be under the circumstances. There is nothing we can do to change it. Now Voltaire and Rousseau did not believe this, but their opposition rested on their belief that the evils of life were brought about by civilization. Man in his natural state is not evil.

Wesley, on the other hand, believes just the opposite. He believes that man in his natural state is evil. But man does not exist in his natural state, for he has the preventing grace of God. He believes, therefore, that something can be done about the world, but it has to be done by God with man's co-operation. It is this part of man's co-operation that accounts for Wesley's constant antipathy to the Calvinistic doctrine of election. Man can do something and man must do something.

From the days of the Oxford Club until his death Wesley was preaching as the heart of his message what William Law had called "A Serious Call to a Devout and Holy Life." The doctrine of Christian perfection, in Wesley's mind, was the heart of the whole matter.

In 1777 he published his "Plain Account of Christian Perfection as Believed and Taught by the Reverend Mr. John Wesley, from the year 1725 to the year 1777." When he put the year 1725 in the title of his *History of Christian Perfection* he apparently meant exactly what he said.

In the year 1725, being in the twenty-third year of my age, I met with Bishop Taylor's "Rules and Exercises of Holy Living and Dying." In reading several parts of the book, I was exceedingly affected; that part in particular which relates to purity of intention. Instantly I resolved to dedicate all my life to God, all my thoughts and words, and actions; being thoroughly convinced, there was no medium; but that every part of my life (not some only) must either be a sacrifice to God, or myself, that is, in effect, to the devil.

Wesley goes on to say that in 1733 (which was before he went to America) he preached at the University of Oxford on "The Circumcision of the Heart"; and he adds:

This was the view of religion I then had, which even then I scrupled not to term *perfection*. This is the view I have of it now, without any material addition or diminution. And what is there here, which any man of understanding, who believes the Bible, can object to?

There is no reference here to Wesley's talk with Peter Boehler or to his "conversion." He does say that in Germany he had a long talk with Arvid Gradin, and he quotes what Gradin gave him as a definition of "the full assurance of faith." This, as we have seen, Wesley translated as "Repose in the blood of Christ; a firm confidence in God, and persuasion of His favour; the highest tranquility, serenity, and peace of mind; with a deliverance from every fleshly desire, and a cessation of all, even inward sins."

According to Wesley, this was the first account he had ever heard from any living man of what he had before learned himself from the oracles of God and had been praying for and expecting for several years. Wesley declares that the first time he put into print his notion of perfection he put it under the indifferent title, "The Character of a Methodist." And he set forth this definition:

A Methodist is one who loves the Lord his God with all his heart, with all his soul, with all his mind, and with all his strength. God is the joy of his heart.... He is therefore happy in God; yea, always happy, as having in him a well of water springing up into everlasting life, and overflowing his soul with peace and joy. Perfect love having now cast out fear, he rejoices evermore.

When I suggested several years ago that Wesley had expected more from his experience of personal faith in Christ, at the instruction of Peter Boehler, than circumstances justified, there were objections raised. But I have never seen the force of the objections. On January 4, 1739, not quite a year after Wesley's conversion, he writes, "I affirm I am not a Christian now . . . that I am not a Christian at this day I as assuredly know as that Jesus is the Christ." His reasons are that he does not have the fruits of the Spirit, love, peace, and joy.[13]

It was this experience which probably lent emphasis to Wesley's protest against Count Zinzendorf's refusal to admit any possible Christian Perfection except as imputed.[14] Niebuhr sees this as exhibiting the contrast between "perfectionist spirituality" and the Reformation. In a sense this is true, but I doubt that it is true in the sense that Wesley meant.[15] Wesley's "inherent" perfection, as Zinzendorf called it, was not quite what the "perfectionist" sects have made it. He was in line rather with the saints of the historic church in their search for perfection.

In his methods Wesley did not neglect some of the traditional ways of the saints of old. In his devotion to Thomas à Kempis and to other Catholic writers he witnessed to his belief that inward and outward purity demanded something of the asceticism traditionally attributed to Catholic sainthood. Wesley talked much about his opposition to the mystics, but he was thinking in terms of a particular from of mysticism. In a wider definition of that word, he himself was a mystic. At least, he was if a consciousness of the divine is a mystical trait.

But Wesley had learned the value of that self-surrender which William James regarded as so important in conversion. The water bears you up when you do not struggle against it. Wesley's search for Christian Perfection involved continuous walking in a larger world which one perceives by faith. All the years after his discovery of the power of self-surrender and the great comfort of the belief that God forgives us individually, Wesley believed that the end of the road toward Perfection might come suddenly—by faith. He even counted up the number of those in London who believed that they had arrived. They all claimed instantaneous achievements of the second blessing.[16]

Perhaps the greatest characteristic of early Methodism was its preaching of Christian Perfection, granted that it gave countenance to fanatical groups and ideas by so doing. Granted that Wesley's own cautious statements that most people[17] do not receive this holiness until the hour and article of death and his other moderating statements were little understood or heeded. Yet there was an air of expectancy about the movement. In Wesley's mind it went back to 1725. It included his own experience of the power of faith. It included his larger definition of faith.

In his sermon, "Walking by Sight and by Faith," he asks, "Do you walk by faith?" He explains his meaning:

I do not ask, whether you curse, or swear, or profane the Sabbath, or live in any outward sin. I do not ask, whether you do good, more or less; or attend all the ordinances of God. But, suppose you are blameless in all these respects, I ask, in the name of God, by what standard you judge of the value of things?[18]

Faith is "not only trust, it is also the opening of man's inward eyes by the grace of God, so that he no longer walks by sight but by apprehension of a new world of values." In this search for the ultimate of the Christian's privileges man should walk by faith in this more general sense and seek the End in the appointed way.

Professor McNeill is right in calling it a "vulgar error" to suppose that the Puritans were morose people. But it is also true that Puritans and Methodists alike have sometimes made religion a sorrowful thing. Both have at times enjoyed their woes. Nevertheless, there is a distinct difference in the types of piety in one point. The Methodists may have been a noisy people, but it was usually intended for a joyful noise. "Shouting" was sometimes a crude form of emotionalism, but it was usually intended as an expression of praise.

When Christian in *Pilgrim's Progress* came to the edge of Jordan, he was still uncertain and fearful. Hopeful tried to cheer him, but Christian replied as he waded into the cold waters: "Ah! my friend, . . . I shall not see the land that flows with milk and honey; and with that a great darkness and horror fell upon Christian, so that he could not see before him."

Nor was it only in the hour and article of death that

the ideal pilgrim found himself in doubt. Professor T. R. Glover, the public orator of Cambridge, one of the great religious writers of our time, has a little essay on "The Pilgrim,"[19] in which there is a paragraph which perhaps more beautifully and more accurately describes the pilgrim attitude than anything else in our language:

His gaze is fixed on something far off, towards which he will go; but if you ask him what he sees, it seems the perspective glass shook in his hand, and he could not look steadily—he thinks he saw something like a gate, and some of the glory of the place—so that, if you roundly tell him there is no such place, the best he can say is that he has heard and believes there is; he does not know.[20]

Obviously the Methodist who came talking about assurance was not a pilgrim in Bunyan's sense. The pilgrim at best could produce Hopeful and Faithful, but he would not use the audacious language of the sons of Wesley. It is not easy in this century to translate Wesley's talk about assurance, or the witness of the spirit, into language which we can understand. Indeed Wesley himself in his later years regretted his earlier dogmatism, but the idea is understandable however one defines it or explains it. The Methodist was not a pilgrim stumbling on his way, hoping but not sure. He was singing:

> We who in Christ believe
>   That He for us hath died,
> We all His unkown peace receive,
>   And feel His blood applied.
>
> Exults our rising soul,
>   Disburdened of her load,
> And swells unutterably full
>   Of glory and of God.

Moreover, the Methodist was no "pilgrim of the

lonely road," to use the title that Gaius Glenn Atkins
used twenty-odd years ago as the title for a book.
The Methodists had a fellowship and the fellowship
was important. We sometimes quote Wesley out of all
context. When he said that there is no religion but social
religion we get a meaning borrowed from twentieth-
century controversies about the social gospel. Wesley
meant nothing of the sort. He could not conceive of
the normal man proceeding except in fellowship with
his brethren. It is true that he made great allowances
for individuals, but he took it for granted that a man
needs his brethren and his brethren need him.

Indeed, Wesley took the doctrine of the Communion
of Saints in the sense of the earlier church: part of the
hosts have crossed the flood and part are crossing now.
The Christian belongs to a great company, some in this
world and some in the next. The Methodist fellowship
was a very real thing, and Wesley's insistence upon it
removes him from those who conceive of the Christian's
way as that of a "lonely pilgrim" who is trying to find
his road in a dark and uncertain world.

When you have made due allowance, therefore, for
the eighteenth century's love of meditating among the
tombs, and when you have remembered the nature of
the Pilgrim's faith, which at its best could hear only the
trumpets as they sounded on the other side, consider if
you will the Methodists.

I confess that for a long time I did not quite understand the significance of the fact that Susannah Wesley
on her deathbed asked for her children to stand around
her and sing. Nor did I quite understand the further significance of Wesley's dying words: "I'll praise, I'll
praise." I knew, of course, that he was quoting Isaac
Watts's hymn, but I had not connected it with the Methodist joy. He was trying to sing this stanza:

> I'll praise my Maker while I've breath,
> And when my voice is lost in death,
>   Praise shall employ my nobler powers;
> My days of praise shall ne'er be past,
>   While life, and thought, and being last,
>   Or Immortality endures.

The truth is that you cannot understand the peculiar nature of the Methodist message unless you understand its note of confidence in an age of dissolution, its preoccupation, not with the other world but with the duties of man in this world and with the ordinance of a living institution, which are the actual means of grace. Nor can you understand what the Methodist Evangel was in this era of dissolution unless you remember the emphasis upon joy, the singing message of these people who went about throughout the breadth and corners of the three kingdoms and across the seas at a time when so few people had anything to sing about.

To be sure, every Christian is in a sense a pilgrim, a stranger in a strange land, a colonist of a better world. As Glover puts it in the little essay which I have quoted: "A pilgrim through shams, delusions, vanities, and compromises." But there is a difference in this sense of pilgrimage.

In *Pilgrim's Progress* when Christian had crossed the river and had divested himself of his mortal garments he heard the sound of trumpets, and when Mr. Valiant-for-truth passed over "all the trumpets sounded for him on the other side."

These are great words, among the greatest in our Christian heritage. But I should like most humbly to suggest that the contribution of the Methodists to a changing world was largely in their belief that they on this side of the dark waters caught the sound of trumpets.

NOTES

References to Wesley material are to the following editions:

Journal, Standard Edition, ed. Nehemiah Curnock (8 vols.; London: Epworth Press, 1909-16).

Wesley's Standard Sermons, ed. Edward H. Sugden (2 vols.; London: Epworth Press, 1921). Contains the first fifty-three sermons.

The Letters of the Rev. John Wesley, ed. John Telford (8 vols.; London: Epworth Press, 1931).

The Works of the Rev. John Wesley (14 vols.; London: Wesleyan Conference Office, 1872).

The Poetical Works of John and Charles Wesley, col. and ar. by G. Osborn (13 vols.; London: Wesleyan Conference Office, 1868-72).

The Works of John and Charles Wesley: A Bibliography (2nd ed.; London: Methodist Publishing House, 1906). This is the standard Wesleyan bibliography.

The *Proceedings* of the Wesley Historical Society (London) are a must for any Wesley student.

CHAPTER ONE

1. *Works,* VII, 424-25.
2. *Ibid.,* pp. 442-23.
3. John S. Simon, *John Wesley and the Methodist Societies* (London: Epworth Press, 1923), pp. 103-4.
4. Umphrey Lee, *John Wesley and Modern Religion* (Nashville: Cokesbury Press, 1936), p. 113.
5. Umphrey Lee, "Freedom from Rigid Creed," in William K.

Anderson (ed.), *Methodism* (Nashville: Methodist Publishing House, 1947).

6. G. C. Coulton, *Five Centuries of Religion* (Cambridge: Cambridge University Press, 1923), I, 540.
7. *Works*, III, 37.
8. Edward Eggleston, *The Circuit Rider* (New York: J. B. Ford & Co., 1874), p. 101.
9. "Christian Perfection," *Works*, III, 130.
10. *Ibid.*, p. 53.
11. *Works*, VIII, 312-13.

CHAPTER TWO

1. *Journal*, VI, 502.
2. Corra Harris, *A Circuit Rider's Widow* (New York, 1916), pp 23-24.
3. *Works*, XI, 490.
4. *Ibid.*, VIII, 318.
5. *Ibid.*, pp. 321-22.
6. Nolan B. Harmon, *The Rites and Ritual of Episcopal Methodism* (Nashville: Publishing House of the M. E. Church, South, 1926), p. 48.
7. *Journal*, V, 26.
8. Leslie F. Church, *The Early Methodist People* (New York: Philosophical Library, 1949), p. 150. The discussion in chap. iv, "Fellowship," is valuable to all students of early Methodism.
9. John Telford (ed.), *Wesley's Veterans* (London: Charles H. Kelly, 1912), III, 37.
10. *The Journal of the Rev. Charles Wesley, M.A.* (London: Wesleyan Methodist Book-Room, n.d.), I, 324.
11. Eggleston, *op. cit.*
12. Lee, *John Wesley and Modern Religion*, pp. 95-96.
13. *Letters*, I, 41.

CHAPTER THREE

1. Quoted in Leslie F. Church, *More About the Early Methodist People* (London: Epworth Press, 1949), p. 14.
2. J. E. Rattenbury, *The Conversion of the Wesleys* (London: Epworth Press, 1938), p. 118.
3. *Journal*, I, 142.
4. *Ibid.*, II, 49.
5. *Works*, II, 370.
6. *Letters*, I, 22.
7. J. E. Hutton, *A History of the Moravian Church* (London, 1909), pp. 288-89.

8. Rattenbury, *op. cit.*, p. 130.
9. Lee, *John Wesley and Modern Religion*, pp. 165-66.

CHAPTER FOUR

1. H. R. McAdoo, *The Structure of Caroline Moral Theology* (London: Longmans, Green, 1949), p. 1.
2. John C. Bowmer, *The Sacrament of the Lord's Supper in Early Methodism* (London, 1951), p. 204.
3. *Letters*, V, 264.
4. *Works*, X, 484.
5. *Journal*, I, 419.
6. A. W. Harrison, *Beginnings of Arminianism* (London: University of London Press, 1926), pp. 161-65.
7. Norman Sykes, *The English Religious Tradition* (London, 1953), p. 38.
8. A. W. Ballard, in *Church Quarterly Review*, CXLI (October-December, 1945), p. 100.
9. McAdoo, *op. cit.*, p. 2.
10. Samuel Wesley, *The History of the New Testament Attempted in Verse* (London, 1701), p. 272.
11. *Journal*, I, 16.
12. *Church Quarterly Review*, CXVII (January, 1934), 288.
13. *Notes on the New Testament* (Nashville: Publishing House of the M. E. Church, South, 1894), p. 490.
14. "Arminius" in *Methodist Quarterly Review*, XI (1857), p. 358.
15. Sermon LXXXV, *Works*, VI, 512.
16. Reinhold Niebuhr, *The Nature and Destiny of Man* (New York: Charles Scribner's Sons, 1941), I, 263.
17. *Letters*, IV, 172.
18. *Ibid.*, p. 126.
19. John Fletcher, *Checks to Antinomianism* (New York: Hunt & Eaton, 1891), I, 50.
20. *Letters*, VI, 202-3.
21. *Journal*, V, 244.
22. *Sermons*, I, 242.
23. *Ibid.*
24. *Ibid.*, pp. 248 ff.
25. *Journal*, Aug. 24, 1776.
26. *Ibid.*, Sept. 14, 1785.
27. Note by Sugden, *Sermons*, I, 250.

CHAPTER FIVE

1. *Journal*, II, 229-30.
2. *Ibid.*, III, 232.

3. Umphrey Lee, *The Lord's Horseman* (New York: Century Co., 1928), pp. 231-34. The reference occurs in the chapter called "The Spirit of '76."

4. Jerome, Ep. CXLVI, I. 1. 6.

5. Quoted by Paul Elmer More and Frank Leslie Cross, *Anglicanism* (London: Society for Promoting Christian Knowledge, 1935), p. 141, and requoted by E. R. Fairweather and R. F. Hettlinger, *Episcopacy and Reunion* (London: Mowbray, 1952), p. 81. See also Bowmer, *op. cit.*, pp. 158-59.

CHAPTER SIX

1. Niebuhr, *op. cit.*, II, 170.

2. See the discussion in Martin Schmidt, *John Wesley* (Frankfurt, 1953), I, 268 ff.

3. *Proceedings of the Eighth Ecumenical Conference* (London: Epworth Press, 1952), p. 98.

4. John T. McNeill, *Modern Christian Movements* (Philadelphia: Westminster Press, 1954), p. 79.

5. *Ibid.*, p. 81.

6. *Ibid.*

7. *Journal*, III, 285-86.

8. Preface to Vol. VII of Christian Library, *Works*, XIV, 229.

9. *Works*, VI, 263.

10. Lee, *John Wesley and Modern Religion*, p. 252.

11. Basil Willey, *The Eighteenth Century Background* (London, 1940), p. 55.

12. *Ibid.*

13. *Journal*, I, 125-26.

14. *Ibid.*, II, 487.

15. Niebuhr, *op. cit.*, II, 174.

16. James mistook these for converts in the usual sense. *Varieties of Religious Experience* (New York: Longmans, Green, 1902), p. 227.

17. Not all, as Niebuhr seems to understand in *op. cit.*, II, 175, n. 15.

18. *Works*, VII, 256-63.

19. T. B. Glover, *The Pilgrim* (London: Student Christian Movement, 1921).

20. *Ibid.*, pp. 16-17.

INDEX